# 10
## BEST
### Teaching
### Practices

Donna Walker TILESTON

# 10 BEST Teaching Practices

*How*
Brain Research, Learning Styles,
and Standards Define Teaching
Competencies

**CORWIN PRESS, INC.**
A Sage Publications Company
Thousand Oaks, California

*For information:*

Corwin Press, Inc.
A Sage Publications Company
2455 Teller Road
Thousand Oaks, California 91320
E-mail: order@corwinpress.com

Sage Publications Ltd.
6 Bonhill Street
London EC2A 4PU
United Kingdom

Sage Publications India Pvt. Ltd.
M-32 Market
Greater Kailash I
New Delhi 110 048 India

Printed in the United States of America

**Library of Congress Cataloging-in-Publication Data**

Tileston, Donna Walker.
        Ten best teaching practices: How brain research, learning styles, and
    standards define teaching competencies / by Donna Walker Tileston.
            p.   cm.
        Includes bibliographical references (p. 75) and index.
        ISBN 0-7619-7584-5 (cloth : alk. paper)
        ISBN 0-7619-7585-3 (pbk. : alk. paper)
        1.  Effective teaching—United States.   2.  Learning.   3.  Educational
    innovations—United States.   4.  Educational change—United States.
    I.  Title: 10 best teaching practices.   II.  Title.
        LB1775.2 .T54   2000
        371.102—dc21                                                    00-008490

This book is printed on acid-free paper.

        02   03   04   05   10   9   8   7   6   5   4   3

| | |
|---|---|
| *Corwin Editorial Assistant:* | Catherine Kantor |
| *Production Editor:* | Denise Santoyo |
| *Editorial Assistant:* | Victoria Cheng |
| *Typesetter/Designer:* | Lynn Miyata |

# Contents

# Preface

*The ultimate source of exceptional performance is exceptional learning. Therefore, the question is how can we best produce exceptional learning in young people? How can we make exceptional learning unexceptional?*

—Lawrence Hooper

We live in a time in which a revolution in education is occurring. Through brain research and technology, we have unlocked many of the reasons why some children experience so much difficulty in learning. We know more about effective teaching practices than at any other time in history. Through technological advances, we have a whole world as our resource base. In addition, teachers are finally being empowered to make the choices that affect their classrooms.

Although we have tremendous resources available to us, schools have been slow to use that information to change the way classrooms are conducted. We live in an age in which vast amounts of information must be assimilated, synthesized, and communicated, yet too many schools continue to teach with the methods of the 1950s . . . rote memorization of dates, places, and facts that are quickly forgotten after "the test." It is no wonder that we are losing our students and that they enter the world ill prepared for the information explosion. As we shift to a new age and a vastly different approach in the way businesses operate, we must also shift our thinking. The National Association for Supervision and Curriculum Development (1999a) says, "In 10 years, there will be two kinds of people: the well educated and the hardly employable." Knowledge and technology will be the great equalizers of this millennium. Education has a responsibility to see that students have, at a minimum, the knowledge base they need to be "players" on a level playing field.

This book is written to incorporate the brain research, learning styles information, and the issue of standards into a classroom instructional model. It is not intended to be a technical manual on the brain; the bookstores are filled with books that do a good job of giving us the technical research. Rather, this book is a look at the application of the brain research and how it can be applied to the classroom. We have wonderful research available to us, but reading and discussing it is not enough: We must get it to the people who can benefit the most—our students. We will reach our students only when we incorporate the knowledge base we have into classroom practices.

I have identified 10 teaching practices that have tremendous power in the classroom when we incorporate the best of research with their implementation. These teaching strategies are based on the best research in the field and on real classroom experience by practitioners. Thirteen years ago I began a dynamic field study on the factors that enhance learning and the factors that impede it. Along with a group of teachers, I used the research that was available at that time to help restructure a school in trouble. Positive results could be seen almost immediately and have been sustained over the years. Today, the school that once had low test scores, a high drop-out rate, and many discipline problems enjoys some of the highest test scores in the state, SAT and ACT scores well above the state and national average, and low incidences of discipline problems. What is significant about this study is that the results have been sustained over time—it was not a one-shot quick fix but a systemic process that has grown. The new research on how the brain learns has validated the structures that we put in place and built over the past 13 years.

I am writing this book for educators, to tell you that success is possible in your school. In the chapters that follow, I will examine 10 practices that are essential if we are to make education meaningful and rich. It is a process that takes time, training, resources, and commitment, but it is worth it because it raises the quality of life for kids.

Chapter 1 looks at the importance of a climate that is enriched and emotionally supportive. The brain research on the effects of climate and the brain's capacity to learn is critical. Not only can we reverse the effects of an early negative environment but, according to Sousa (1995), we can actually increase the IQ scores of students by as much as 20 points by enhancing the environment for learning. I consider this chapter to be critical, because if we cannot create a climate in which all students feel physically and emotionally secure, the rest doesn't matter.

Chapter 2 addresses the need for a wide repertoire of teaching techniques so that all students, regardless of learning modality, will be successful. Schools of the past taught mainly to the auditory learners; schools of the future must teach to all learners. New research shows that as much as 80% of the classroom may be made up of students who don't learn auditorily (Sousa, 1999). We must examine not only the three modalities for incoming information, but the rhythm of the teaching as well. The attention span of the brain follows a rhythm that, if incorporated into the time frame of teaching, ensures greater response from students.

Chapter 3 looks at the critical element of connections or transfers in learning. The brain is a seeker of connections and where they do not exist, there is chaos. Our job as educators is to build on connections that already exist and to help create connections where there are none. This chapter offers hope to the parents, teachers, and students as they search for ways to put learning into long-term memory.

Chapter 4 is an investigation into the workings of the memory system. How does the brain decide what to toss and what to keep? More important, how can we take this new knowledge to the classroom? All of us, as educators, have experienced those agonizing moments when we realized that although we taught our hearts out, the students just didn't "get it." With the mystery of how we learn and remember solved, teachers of the future have the opportunity to make learning more meaningful than at any other time in history.

Chapter 5 looks at the need to provide motivating, challenging work in the classroom. The days of meaningless busywork must be brought to a close. Time is too precious a commodity to waste in the classroom. Our students will enter a world in which computers can do rote memory tasks. We must prepare them for the things computers cannot do—problem solving, complex thinking, and collaboration.

Chapter 6 is a discussion of the power of true collaborative learning. In the global world, the need for articulation skills, the ability to work with a variety of people, and the ability to collaborate on problem solving is critical. What a wonderful gift to give to our students! Studies from Marian Diamond (1998) show that we thrive when we learn in social settings.

Chapter 7 discusses the importance of success for all learners. We must take a hard look at student data in its desegregated form. We must look at cultural differences and the research on what works and what does not. It's time to bring in the experts and it is time to be honest about what is not working.

Chapter 8 identifies what authentic assessment is and what it is not. We must move away from assessment that is short term and influenced by rote memory alone to a process that is ongoing and that truly tests long-term memory. We must begin to assess learning in the context of how it is going to be used. Only then can we truly know if students can use the information.

Chapter 9 looks at relevance as it applies to learning. Like climate, this is one of the most powerful areas of influence on how and whether the brain learns and remembers. It is the answer for those who ask, "When are we ever going to use this?"

Chapter 10 is a look into the future to an anytime, anywhere learning space. Technology is an integral part of the home and workplace. Schools must get on board and learn to use productivity tools to lead students to more complex work.

In Chapter 11, I provide some closing remarks based on the findings in this book and on the research from the school that we restructured more than 12 years ago. A true test for any restructured school is whether students are successful and, if so, whether they are successful over time. Students in our school began to show remarkable improvement almost immediately and have built on that success over time. When we began years ago to restructure this school, we did it based on the knowledge available at that time. We did not know many of the things that we now know about how the brain works; we applied what we knew worked for kids and then built on it as new information became available. Our instincts were correct. As these principles apply in that school, I believe they can apply in any school in the country.

## Acknowledgments

The contributions of the following reviewers are gratefully acknowledged:

Sharon Toomey Clark, PhD
Lecturer
California State University, San Bernardino
Claremont, California

Micki M. Caskey
Assistant Professor
Portland State University
Portland, Oregon

Lisa J. Suhr
Instructor
Sabetha Middle School
Hiawatha, Kansas

Tad Watanabe
Department of Mathematics–Instructor
Towson University
Towson, Maryland

# About the Author

*D*onna **Walker Tileston** is a veteran teacher of 27 years, a published author, and a full-time consultant. She is the president of Walker Tileston Consulting, which provides services to schools throughout the United States and Canada. She is the author of *Strategies for Teaching Differently: On the Block or Not* (1998) and *Innovative Strategies of the Block Schedule* (1999).

She received her BA from the University of North Texas, her MA from East Texas State University, and her PhD from Texas A&M University, Commerce. She can be reached through her Internet Web site at *dwtileston.com* or by email: dwtileston@yahoo.com.

To my sons,
Christopher Scott McBrayer and Kevin Lane McBrayer,
and in memory of their brother,
Chad Michael McBrayer.

# Creating an Enriched and Emotionally Supportive Environment

*Except for those who live in deepest poverty, the psychological needs—love, power, freedom, and fun—take precedence over the survival needs, which most of us are able to satisfy. All our lives we search for ways to satisfy our needs for love, belonging, caring, sharing, and cooperation. If a student feels no sense of belonging in school, no sense of being involved in caring and concern, that child will pay little attention to academic subjects.*

—W. Glasser (1994), "Teach Students
What They Will Need in Life"

Environment is so important that none of the other techniques discussed will be really effective unless the issues of enrichment and support are addressed first. In a world full of broken relationships, broken promises, and broken hearts, a strong supportive relationship is important to students. While we cannot control the students' environments outside the classroom, we have tremendous control over their environment for 7 hours each day. We have the power to create positive or negative images about education, to develop an enriched environment, and to become the catalysts for active learning. We now know that how we feel about education has great impact on how the brain reacts to it. Emotion and cognitive learning are not separate entities; they work in tandem with one another.

In order to understand the importance of enrichment and support, we must examine how learning takes place in the brain. Two types of cells, neuron and glial (meaning glue), are of great importance to learning. When neurons communicate with one another, learning takes place (Sousa, 1995). Neurons communicate through their parts: the *cell body*, the *dendrites*, and the *axon*. Springer (1999) uses a simple analogy (Figure 1.1) to explain the three parts:

> The cell body is represented by the palm of your hand. Information enters the cell body through appendages called dendrites, represented by your fingers. Just as you wiggle your fingers, your dendrites are constantly moving as they seek new information. If the neuron needs to send a message to another neuron, the message is sent through the axon. Your wrist and forearm represent the axon.

When a neuron sends information down to its axon to communicate with another neuron, it never actually touches the other neuron. The message goes from the axon of the sending neuron to the dendrite of the receiving neuron by "swimming" through a space called a *synapse*. As the neurons make connections, the brain grows dendrites and strengthens the synapses. Glial cells are support cells that hold the neurons together and act as filters to keep harmful substances out of the neurons. They may have great significance in regard to how well we think. When examinations of Albert Einstein's brain tissue were conducted, scientists found that he showed more glial cells per neuron than the average person (Sousa, 1995).

Although the goal in education is to promote learning, sometimes outside factors inhibit the process. One of these inhibitors is stress, and a common reason for stress in students is threat. Jenson (1998) says, "threat impairs brain cells. Threat also changes the body's chemistry and impacts learning." As a matter of fact, when people experience stress over periods of time they may suffer some damage to the dendritic growth. Stress chemicals act on the hypocampus, the part of the brain that filters and helps to store long-term factual memories. Some examples of threat in the classroom include anything that embarrasses a student, unrealistic deadlines, a student's inability to speak a language, inappropriate learning styles, and an uncomfortable classroom culture (Jenson, 1998).

Years ago, I was involved in a restructuring project in a high school that proved to me the enormous impact of positive climate on student learning. Our faculty had come to a point of desperation . . . we knew students were not learning at a quality level and we knew they did not want to come to school. Our high drop-out rate was proof. We understood how the students felt because we too were burned out. Our test scores were average at best; we had a high drop-out rate, a fledgling attendance rate, and discipline problems. So, we came together and made a list of all the things we thought were wrong with school and a list of the things that were keeping us from being the kind of learning place we wanted to be. We did our homework. We studied the research and we called in the experts. We were actively involved in more than 15 days of training on the factors that enhance learning and the factors that

**FIGURE 1.1.** Analogy of the Structure of the Neuron

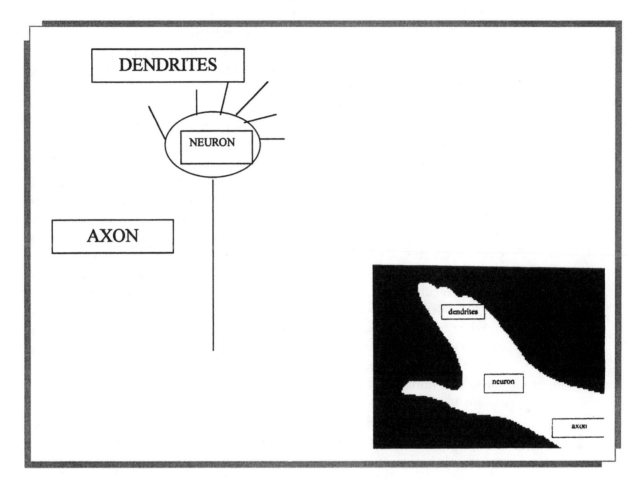

impede it. As we came to know more about how children learn, we changed our attitude about teaching and learning, and we reinvented our school into the kind of place we believed school should be. When our students came back in the fall it was to an entirely different kind of school. On the first day of school, we stood in front of our classes and gave students a pep talk that would make any coach proud. We talked about how we believed in our students. We encouraged them to do their best work and we promised them that we would be the best teachers we had ever been. We told them that there would be no more "gotchas" in our school, that they would always be told what they needed to do to be successful in our classrooms—and if they did it, they would be successful. We quit teaching as if we were the all-knowing scribes and made the students active participants in the learning. We created real-world applications to the learning and we told students up front what the learning had to do with their world. We encouraged creativity, connections to the learning, and reflective thinking. We created a place where learning was respected and nourished—and we all thrived.

In October of that year, we gave our state exam, which students must pass in order to graduate. As a faculty, we told ourselves not to be discouraged if the scores were not improved over the prior year. After all, we had been teaching differently for only 2 months and there was no way we could make up for the lack of knowledge in 2 months. When the scores came back, there was so much improvement that we thought it was a fluke. In the past, only 28% of our at-risk students had mastered every part of the test on the first try. When our tests came back, 67% of our at-risk students mastered every part of the state test. We were baffled. We knew we could not have taught these students that much material in only 2 months!

In the winter, while in Austin, I attended a seminar on brain research conducted by Madeline Hunter. She talked first about the research of the 1970s, called the Placebo Effect, in which a group of people were told that they were being given penicillin for a virus when, in fact, they were being given a placebo. Regardless, one third of them got well. Her new research showed that if the doctor giving the placebo believes that he is giving the group penicillin, and if he convinces the group of this, more than half of them will get well. I knew, then, what had happened to our at-risk students. For the first time, as a group, we believed that all kids could learn, we convinced the students of that fact, and more than half of them—67%—got well. What a powerful influence emotion is on the brain. When we begin to tap into that power in schools, remarkable things are possible.

In his book *How the Brain Learns*, David Sousa (1995) talks about the influence of emotion on the brain. He says that emotional responses can actually diminish the brain's ability to process cognitive information:

> We have all had experiences when anger, fear of the unknown, or joy quickly overcame our rational thoughts. This override of conscious thought can be strong enough to cause temporary inability to talk . . . or move. This happens because the hippocampus is susceptible to stress hormones which can inhibit cognitive functioning and long-term memory.

Students who feel threatened in the classroom, whether physically or emotionally, are operating in a survival mode, and while learning can take place in that mode, it is with much difficulty. If a student feels that no matter what he does he can never please the teacher; if a student feels that no matter how hard he tries he can never understand the subject—whether the threat is real or perceived—he will not ever be able to reach his potential in that environment.

Another aspect of creating a positive environment is sometimes referred to as "enriched environment." Marion Diamond (1988), distinguished researcher and national lecturer on brain research from the University of California at Berkeley, has conducted powerful research on the effects of rats raised in enriched and in impoverished environments. The implications for the classroom are far reaching.

In one study, Dr. Diamond and her colleagues placed 12 rats in a large cage that contained rat toys for climbing and running (enriched environment). A similar cage contained 12 rats but no toys (impoverished environment). The rats in the enriched environment produced more and thicker dendrite connections than the rats in the impoverished environment. Thus the conclusion was drawn that the enriched environment enhanced the growth of dendrites. When a neuron wants to send a message to another neuron, it does so by sending the message through its axon to the dendrite of another neuron, thus a connection is made. As connections are made, the brain grows dendrites and brain growth occurs (Diamond, 1988).

In another part of the study, a young rat was placed in an enriched environment with older rats. The older rats would not allow the young rat to play with the rat toys, and it was discovered that the young rat, deprived of enrichment, did not grow any new dendrites while the older rats continued to produce new growth (Diamond, 1988).

Other studies support the work of Diamond and the conclusions about the importance of an enriched environment. University of Illinois researcher William Greenbough found through 30 years of research that he could increase the number of connections in animal brains by 25% just by exposing them to an enriched environment (Greenbough & Anderson, 1991).

Craig Ramey from the University of Alabama conducted a similar study with children who came from an impoverished environment. In his study, he exposed half of the children to an enriched environment. The children in the enriched environment showed IQ scores 20 points higher than the children who were not exposed to an enriched environment (Jenson, 1995).

What are the implications for the classroom? First, we can conclude that an enriched environment is better for the developing brain. Jenson (1998) believes that enrichment in the classroom comes primarily from challenge and feedback. He warns that too little challenge in the classroom breeds boredom and that too much can intimidate. Challenge should be filtered so that it provides stimulating and fun experiences that match the ability level of the student without causing frustration. Jenson (1998) says that feedback should be a part of the learning about every 30 minutes. Feedback, however, is not always from the teacher. Feedback takes on many forms including peer evaluations, journal writing, predicting activities, group presentations, and rubrics. Springer (1999) adds that an enriched environment means that students are actively involved in the learning, not passive receivers. Just as the young rat did not thrive when not allowed to participate, so children who merely sit on the sidelines while the teacher acts as the sole player in the education process will not learn at the level that would have been possible had they participated. It is the teacher who will grow new dendrites.

Other factors that help to create an enriched and supportive environment include the following: A sense of belonging, a high level of support for achievement, a sense of empowerment, more on-ramps, an advocate for every student, and resiliency in students.

### A Sense of Belonging

All of us want to belong somewhere. We want to feel we are a part of the experience and that we are accepted. When students do not feel accepted, for whatever reason, they are more likely to find negative places to belong. That is what helps to keep gangs active in our students' lives. Gangs and other negative influences fill a need that so often is not met in positive settings. As educators we must create an environment in which students feel safe and accepted, an environment in which we are all learners together and where we feel a sense of togetherness—one where there are no "gotchas." Students are told up front what they must do to be successful and then we are faithful and hold them only to the criteria that we set. Give students the tools they need to be successful and then allow them the opportunity to fulfill that success. I have never met a student who wanted to fail. Hanson and Childs (1998) published the results of a survey given to students in Chicago, Houston, and Norfolk about what most concerned them about school. The number one concern (51.77%) was school failure. We have the power to elevate or eliminate that concern. Martin Haberman (1996) says, "Star teachers lead youngsters to believe 'It's you and me against the material.' Quitter and failure teachers lead students to believe, 'It's the material and me against you.'"

### A High Level of Support for Achievement

Teachers and students expect quality work; they will not accept anything less. We insult students when we accept mediocre work. Students are given very clear directions about what they must do to be successful, they are given the tools they need in order to make that success possible, and they are given the time to do it right. The expectation is consistent throughout the school; students cannot turn in shoddy work in one classroom and then be expected to do their best in another. A friend of mine who is a powerful math teacher has a sign in her room that says, "I promise to be the best math teacher you have ever had; will you promise to be the best math student you have ever been?" Students who have never before been successful in mathematics are successful in her classroom. It's a matter of attitude.

Kotulak (1996) says,

Now, thanks to a recent revolution in molecular biology and new imaging techniques, researchers believe that genes, the chemical blueprints of life, establish the framework of the brain, but then the environment takes over and provides the customized finishing touches. They work in tandem. The genes provide the building blocks and the environment acts like an on-the-job foreman providing instructions for final construction.

The environment in which students learn has far-reaching effects on how well and how much students learn. We now know through studies such as those at the University of Alabama that a positive learning environment can actually help elevate IQ scores. Kotulak (1996) goes on to quote Dr. Fredrick Goodwin, the former director of the National Institute of Mental Health (NIMH), who says, "You can't make a 70 IQ person into a 120 IQ person but you can change their IQ measure in different ways, perhaps as much as 20 points up or down, based on their environment."

## A Sense of Empowerment

All of us feel better about our circumstances when we feel we have some power over what happens to us. Students should have input into the decisions that affect their lives daily. Look at the policies and rules in your school and ask, "How many are necessary, and how many no longer apply but are in place because at some point in the past they were deemed necessary?" In the school that we changed so dramatically, we went to zero rules and rebuilt our list of rules based on the true needs of the students, staff, and community at that time. It was amazing how many rules were on the books simply because over time no one had bothered to ask if they were really necessary. Hanson and Childs (1998) say, "In a school with a positive climate, policies encourage and seek a win/win result." Covey (1989) describes win/win as, "A frame of mind and heart that constantly seeks mutual benefit in all human interactions. A win/win solution means that all parties feel good about the decision and feel committed to the action plan. Win/win sees life as a cooperative, not a competitive arena." In the classroom, we empower students when we involve them in the class rules and when we give them choices in the assignments. As a matter of fact, any time we give students choices, we give them power.

In our restructured high school, I saw an amazing application of this principle of giving students choices. We had a nagging problem with discipline; there were fights in the hallway every day. As a matter of fact, the principal at the time said that he watched certain groups of students all the time, waiting for the next fight. Our schedule included a 15-minute activity period designed to give students a chance to go to the library, go by a teacher's room to leave an assignment, or just to give the students a break to have a soft drink and to speak to their friends. Students loved it; we hated it. That was the time when we had the largest number of individual discipline problems. Out of frustration, the principal took the 15-minute break out of the daily schedule. A group of students, appointed by the general student body, visited the principal to see if there was any way they could get their break time back into the schedule. He told them that he would make a deal with them. He said that as long as there were no fights, no acts of vandalism of school property, and no litter after break or lunch they could have the break. However, anytime an adult had to break up a fight, anytime there was an act of vandalism, and anytime the hallway was left with debris after the break they would lose the break for 3 days. Signs in the hallway informed students whether break was on for the day. Over time, there was a dramatic change in the students' behavior; they patrolled between classes and before and after school, and the difference in the school was remarkable. For some students, the 15-minute break was the only time during the school day that they saw their boyfriends or girlfriends and "woe unto" anyone who started a fight and caused the entire school to miss the break. One afternoon, I was seated in one of the student's desks waiting for the bell to ring when I heard a commotion outside the door. There were no teachers in sight and since I was seated at a student desk, no one knew I was there. Two students were getting ready to fight. They were glaring at each other and mouthing. The tension was high. Before I could get to the hallway, between 10 and 15 students had gotten between the angry students, pushing them back, talking to them, cooling them off—much the way pro athletes do in a game where a penalty would be crucial. This became the norm in that school, and over time discipline problems became minimal.

## More On-Ramps

Schools provide plenty of opportunities for students to drop out, physically or mentally or both. Metaphorically, these are the off-ramps. What we need are more on-ramps to keep students engaged, in school, and on-track. Schools can provide more on-ramps by providing more choices in offerings, including not only high-level courses that prepare for higher education, but current meaningful studies that lead to vocations. Take a hard look at the course offerings and ask some critical questions. What do students really need to know and be able to do in order to have marketable skills? Is there a segment of the school population that is being left out? Could we team up with community colleges and with major universities to provide more opportunities for our students? Why can't students take courses in high school that will help them complete 2-year associate degree programs? As a matter of fact, most of those courses could be taught through collaboratives with colleges and universities so that students could leave high school with most of the coursework completed. With video conferencing and distance learning capabilities, students can complete high school and some college work prior to graduation.

Next, we provide on-ramps when we provide choices within the curriculum that incorporate different learning styles and multiple intelligences in the process. Independent projects are a primary opportunity to give students choices for products. The teacher who sets the criteria for the work in the class, yet provides choices within that work, does not diminish the quality of the work, but enhances the depth of the learning by giving students opportunities to bring a variety of products to the learning. Because students learn in different modalities—kinesthetic, auditory, and visual—the teacher who teaches with a variety of techniques provides more opportunities for success to his or her students.

Third, schools provide on-ramps when they lead students to know that if they fail, if they make a mistake, if they break a rule, they can overcome it. I am convinced that we could save quite a few students if they knew that a mistake does not mean there is no hope. While I believe that we need to be accountable for the things we do, I also believe that we must not take away a student's hope that he or she can overcome whatever problem is in the way.

## An Advocate for Every Student

I taught in an inner-city high school of 3,000 students in a non-air-conditioned Texas classroom on the third floor. Hardly a day went by without some act of violence, whether it was a student beaten up, a robbery, or slashed tires in the parking lot. I loved my kids; they made tremendous sacrifices just to come to school each day. I learned far more from them than they probably learned from me. One important rule I learned in that environment was that every kid needs an advocate. All kids need to know that someone is looking over their shoulder and knows whether they have been absent too much, whether they are in danger of failure, whether they are on track for graduation, and if they are having problems in the classroom. *Breaking Ranks* (National Association of Secondary School Principals [NASSP], 1996) reminds us,

> During much of this century, reformers sought to shut small schools and herd youngsters into ever-larger schools that styled themselves after the factory model. Experts perceived bigness as a sine qua non of excellence. This paradigm, with its vast array of offerings, represented the epitome of educational progress. But students are not pieces on an assembly line and knowledge is not an inert commodity to pour into vessels like soft-drink syrup in a bottling plant. The impersonal nature of the high school leaves too many youngsters alienated from the learning process.

We know now that the small-school concept is better because it provides the opportunity for teachers and administration to get to know the students personally. Not all of us are in a position to work and learn in small schools, however. In the age of mega schools, there are some creative solutions to providing the small-school experience within the large-school building. Academic teaming, in which teams of teachers are responsible for 100 or fewer students, is one way that we have been able to provide the advocacy needed by students. Under this model, teams meet on a regular weekly, if not daily, basis. Part of the responsibility of the team is to check on the 100 students assigned to see who has been absent too much, who is tardy often, who is a discipline problem, and who is in danger of failure. This team provides support and counseling to these students on an individual basis. The team may meet with other teachers, administrators, support staff, and/or parents on the student's behalf.

Another popular variation of this is the teacher mentor who is assigned from 20 to 25 students for whom he or she is responsible throughout their school years on that campus. In elementary school, these are often called homeroom teachers; at the secondary level, they take on other titles but the concept is the same. In high school, the mentor teacher stays with the same students throughout high school and may take on some of the duties of school orientation with the group. These teachers are critical to setting a positive school climate for the students to whom they are assigned. As we move to a very diverse population, this is especially important in helping to give all students survival skills. Werner and Smith (1992) cite Rutter, who talks about the needs of at-risk children and suggests, "If we want to help vulnerable youngsters we need to focus on the protective processes that bring about changes in life trajectories from risk to adaptation." Rutter includes among them (a) those that reduce the risk impact, (b) those that reduce the likelihood of negative chain reactions, (c) those that promote self-esteem and self-efficacy, and (d) those that open up opportunities. Werner and Smith (1992) explain, "We have seen these processes at work among the resilient children in our study and among those youths that recovered from serious coping problems in young adulthood. They represent the essence of any effective intervention program, whether by professionals or volunteers."

### Resiliency in Students

Young children seem to have a tremendous capacity for "bouncing back" from traumatic and other emotional experiences. That ability is critical to the brain's capacity to function at a quality level. In his book *Inside the Brain*, Ronald Kotulak (1996) talks about the importance of resiliency. "Studies at the University of Chicago on the environmental inputs that may direct the brain down a path of aggression and violence show that the main culprit is stress." Dr. Bruce Perry, a leader in the work at the University of Chicago, who has since moved to the Baylor College of Medicine, says,

> Many children are raised in violent, abusive surroundings of which they have no control. The antidote is giving children a sense of self-worth and teaching them they are not helpless. If there's somebody out there who makes you feel like you're special and important,

then you can internalize that when you're developing your view of the world.

Perry continues, "When you look at children who come out of terrible environments and do well, you find that someone in their lives somehow instilled in them the attitude that they aren't helpless, that they aren't powerless, that they can do something." Payne (1996) cites the work of Feuerstein and colleagues (1980) with children who came from backgrounds of poverty over generations. She says, "For students from generational poverty to learn, a significant relationship must be present." In fact, in the various studies of children who were able to rise above the poverty, all of them could point to a single individual who helped them emotionally.

In their book, *Resiliency in Schools: Making It Happen for Students and Educators,* Nan Henderson and Mike Milstein (1996) list the following characteristics of families, schools, communities, and peer groups that foster resiliency. They do the following:

- Promote close bonds
- Value and encourage education
- Use high warmth/low criticism style of interaction
- Set and enforce clear boundaries (rules, norms, and laws)
- Encourage supportive relationships with many caring others
- Promote sharing of responsibilities, service to others, "required helpfulness"
- Provide access to resources for basic needs of housing, employment, health care, and recreation
- Express high, realistic expectations for success
- Encourage goal-setting and mastery
- Encourage pro-social development of values (like altruism) and life skills (like cooperation)
- Provide leadership, decision making, and other opportunities for meaningful participation
- Appreciate the unique talents of each individual

While we cannot ensure that students have that kind of support outside the school, we have tremendous power to see that they have that support for 7 hours each day.

**In conclusion:** The evidence is so overwhelming that an enriched and emotionally supportive environment is necessary if students and faculty are to grow mentally that to ignore this aspect of education should be considered

**FIGURE 1.2.** Indicators of an Enriched and Emotionally Supportive Environment

| Assessment Tools | Indicators of Success |
|---|---|
| Matrix/rubric | Higher degree of success by students overall |
| Climate surveys | Results show a high satisfaction with school, low stress level, and a belief that grades, assignments, and assessments are fair and equitable. |
| Overall failure rate | Declining |
| Attendance rates | Rising |
| Dropout rates | Low . . . anything higher than 0 is not acceptable |
| Discipline referrals | Declining |
| Course offerings | A wide variety of options that include flexible scheduling where appropriate |
| Teaching methods | Include visual, tactile, and auditory tools |

malpractice. Thirty-plus years of research says that not just rats, but children, thrive in this environment. Perhaps today more than at any other time in history we need to provide an environment for students that is stress reduced and that has as its central goal to be a place to belong. That means that all gifts are valued and that every student has an opportunity to learn without fear of failure or unacceptance. Teachers must begin to view themselves as partners in the learning, as catalysts for the classroom, not the center of the learning. An enriched environment has less to do with posters on the wall and more to do with challenging, stimulating, and fun activities that tantalize the thought processes, raise the oxygen level in the brain, and cause people to want to be there.

Figure 1.2 shows some of the ways that enriched environments can be measured and the indicators of success.

# *Using a Variety of Teaching Strategies That Address Different Learning Styles*

> *Upon the teachers in all high schools falls the responsibility for ensuring that the work that confronts students has the potential to engage them. Even difficult work need not be boring and inaccessible.*
>
> —National Association of Secondary School
> Principals (1996), *Breaking Ranks*

Schools of the past have relied heavily on lecture as a primary teaching method. Lecture assumes that students learn auditorily, yet through brain research we know that most do not learn that way. Only about 20% of students learn auditorily, the other 80% learn either visually or kinesthetically (Sousa, 1997). While lecture has its place in some courses, it should be used only in short segments—20 minutes or less—depending on the age of the student. It is unrealistic to believe that students who are constantly stimulated by the multimedia world will sit for hours each day passively listening to lectures, taking notes, and preparing for a pencil-and-paper exam without dropping out mentally. Life is not a spectator sport; it is an exercise in active involvement, and education should reflect that active involvement. *Breaking Ranks* (National Association of Secondary School Principals, 1996) echoes this belief in stating, "When possible, students should take an active role in their learning rather than as passive recipients of information passed on by textbooks and by teachers who do little more than lecture." This is a very different type of classroom from the one most often found in schools, where teachers are the imparters of knowledge in a lecture format, and students memorize facts and restate them on paper-and-pencil tests. The transition from a traditional teaching and learning format to an active involvement format takes time and commitment. It is, however, worth it because it is better for students.

In a study led by Marion Diamond (Diamond, Scheibel, Murphy, & Harvey, 1985), baby rats and mature rats were placed in the same cage with rat toys. This is the environment identified by Diamond as enriched and is the environment in which rats in other studies showed brain growth. In this study, the older rats did not allow the baby rats the opportunity to use the rat toys. As a result, the baby rats did not grow dendrites, though the mature rats continued to grow dendrites. Diamond concluded that, "It isn't enough for students to be in an enriched environment, they need to help create that environment and be active in it." In order to ensure that all students are actively learning and that classrooms encourage that participation, we must look at learning modalities. There are three primary learning modalities that make up the learners in our classrooms.

The first modality is *auditory*. Auditory learners are those who remember best information that they hear. Information that is auditory is processed and stored in the temporal lobes on the sides of the brain (Jenson, 1998). These students make up about 20% of the classroom. They like lecture, adapt well to it, and tend to be successful in our traditional schools. When I conduct workshops throughout the country, I often ask my audiences to show by raising hands how many are auditory learners. A large number believe that they are auditory. No surprise, they were probably drawn to teaching partly because they were successful in the auditory-based classrooms of the past. Since we tend to teach the way we learn, it is also no surprise that the majority of teachers in classrooms today like lecture as a primary teaching method.

It is important to add that even though these students learn best by hearing, even they grow weary in a straight lecture format. The work of Sousa (1995) and others shows that all of us tend to drop out mentally after 15 or 20 minutes of lecture. In young children, the mental drop-out time is significantly less—about 10 minutes.

A good friend of mine was a high school English teacher for many years. We called her the "lecture queen" because not only did she lecture all day, but she was good at it. When we began to look at research on attention span and on learning modalities, she decided that it was important to incorporate some other teaching techniques into her classroom so she could reach all of the students. About a month after she started teaching in this new way, she stood in front of the class and said, "Don't you just love the way I am teaching this year?" Because she had moved from teaching junior English to senior English, she had some of the same students in her classroom as the year before. One of those students replied, "No, I hate it." She was crushed. "Why?" The student replied, "Do you remember where I sat last year?" She said that she did and pointed to a chair by the windows at the back of the classroom. The student said,

> What you don't know is that last year I came to class each day, got out my notebook and my textbook, set them up in front of me and went to sleep. You see, the girl behind me took great notes and before each test she would Xerox her notes, give them to me and I

**FIGURE 2.1.** The Rhythm of Teaching

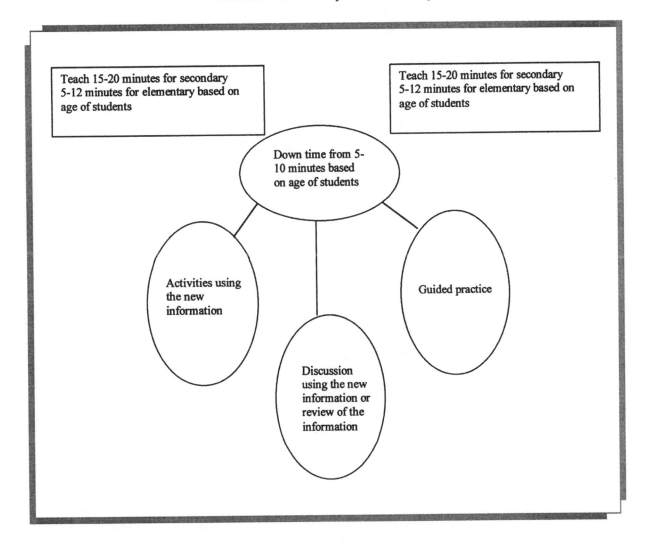

would study from her notes. I would come to class, ace your test, and then go back to sleep. But this year, you are making us be an active part of the learning and I am not getting enough sleep.

Sousa (1995) says that working memory is temporal and deals with information for only a short amount of time before deciding whether to discard it. He identifies the time rate to be about 5 to 10 minutes for pre-adolescents and 10 to 20 minutes for adolescents. Using this information as a guide, secondary teachers should give information for about 15 minutes followed by activities or discussion to reinforce the learning. Elementary teachers would use 7 minutes as their guide. Sousa refers to the teaching segments as prime time. During the first 20 minutes of class, he says, students learn best. New information, information that is of primary importance, should be taught during this time. Figure 2.1 shows how a teacher might use the learning rhythm to enhance student learning.

The second type of learning modality is *visual*. Visual information is processed and stored in the occipital lobe at the back of the brain. Visual learners are those who need a mental model that they can see. I am convinced that we could raise math scores immediately all over this country if we could find a way to show kids how math works. Since the majority of learners are visual learners, we need to find ways to show them visually how math works. When I work with audiences, I give them the following problem to solve: If five people shake hands with each other, how many handshakes is that? Now there is a formula that can be applied to find the answer, and the math people in the audience are quick to work the answer out mathematically. I like to show the answer visually because it opens up a new world to people in the audience who need to see how the math works. My visual answer is in Figure 2.2. All that is left is to add up the handshakes—$4 + 3 + 2 + 1 + 0 = 10$ handshakes.

By the way, the formula is

$$\frac{(x)(x-1)}{2}$$

A more complicated version, such as "One hundred people at the local grocery store shake hands. How many handshakes is that?" is less threatening once we understand how it works.

One of the most effective tools for visual learners is graphic models, sometimes called concrete models. These mental maps help students understand and remember difficult concepts such as sequencing, comparing and contrasting, and classifying. While they are a good teaching strategy for any student, they are important tools for visual students.

Concrete models help students connect or relate new information to prior knowledge. Because they make abstract ideas more visible, they help students understand and remember concepts that are difficult to visualize otherwise. Young students who have difficulty with abstract concepts can be helped by learning to use a set of visual models that take the abstract to the concrete. I believe we can raise the scores of students on standardized tests by giving students concrete models to help them perform difficult skills. I am working with a colleague to produce a series of visual models to help students in our area who are struggling on state and national tests. By taking the information that they know and placing it in a concrete model, students are able to transfer abstract thoughts to concrete ideas more easily. Concrete models can be used at any time during the learning process but are critical in the phase of the lesson in which the teacher wants the students to use the information in some way. This is a time for clarifying ideas for both the student and the teacher—prior to assessment. Other times when concrete models might be used include:

- To introduce a difficult or abstract concept. The old adage "a picture is worth a thousand words" is absolutely true. Many

**FIGURE 2.2.** A Visual Math Solution

Let's identify the five people as persons A, B, C, D, and E, respectively.

Person A does not shake hands with himself, so he shakes with

A + B

A + C

A + D

A + E

That is 4 handshakes.

Person B already has shaken hands with A and does not shake hands with himself, so

B + C

B + D

B + E

That's 3 more handshakes.

*(Continued)*

**FIGURE 2.2.** Continued

Person C already has shaken hands with Persons A and B and does not shake hands with himself, so

C + D

C + E

That's 2 more handshakes.

Person D already has shaken hands with persons A, B, C, and does not shake hands with himself, so

D + E

That's 1 handshake.

Person E already has shaken hands with persons A, B, C, and D. He does not shake hands with himself, so that is 0 handshakes.

students have difficulty with logic problems. A matrix is a visual tool that helps to make this complex skill more manageable.

■ To assess the learning. Instead of having students list items from the learning, give them a choice to mindmap: "Mindmap the key points we discussed in Science class today."

■ As part of an individual or group project. Examples might be mindmaps, flow charts, or attribute webs. When these tools are used at the application level or above, they can be important products in student projects.

■ To demonstrate creativity. Visual students, once they have been exposed to visual models, have little trouble adding creative and elaborative touches to their models.

- To depict relationships between facts and concepts. Cause-and-effect diagrams, fishbones, and Venn diagrams are examples of mental maps that depict relationships.

- To generate and organize ideas for writing. Mindmaps and stratification maps are great tools to help students organize their thoughts before writing.

- To relate new information to prior knowledge

- To store and retrieve information. One of my favorite visuals takes vocabulary words—including in other languages—and draws icons to symbolize the meaning of the words. Students who are visual will see the icons as they retrieve the information from their brains.

- To assess student thinking and learning

- To depict relationships between facts and concepts

Anytime we can help visual learners see the information, we help them process it toward long-term memory.

The third learning modality is *kinesthetic*. Kinesthetic information is stored at the top of the brain in the motor cortex until permanently learned, then it is stored in the cerebellum, the area below the occipital lobe (Jenson, 1998). Kinesthetic learners learn best through movement and touching. In the previous handshake exercise (Figure 2.1), kinesthetic learners would solve the problem by physically shaking hands with four other people and counting the handshakes. Provide opportunities for your class to go outside, to go on field trips, or to role play. In addition, and whenever possible, provide opportunities for them to move around in the classroom, to change groups, or just to stand. The old adage that we think better on our feet is absolutely true. When we stand we increase the flow of fluids to the brain and we do learn better. Take advantage of that in the classroom by having students stand to give answers or to discuss with each other.

**In conclusion:** Although we all record information using all three modalities, most of us have a preference for one of the modalities. Sousa (1995) says that teachers need to understand that students with different sensory preferences will behave differently during learning and that teachers tend to teach the way they learn. That explains, in part, why so many students have trouble learning from one teacher but may learn easily from another. Behavior that has been interpreted to mean the student was not interested in the learning or did not want to learn may, in fact, have only been an indication of inappropriate teaching techniques or a classroom where only one modality was valued. The classroom that is enriched with teaching techniques from all three modalities, and in which new information is given in 15- to 20-minute seg-

**FIGURE 2.3.** Indicators of a Classroom in Which a Variety of Teaching Strategies Are Used to Address Different Learning Styles

| Evaluation Tools | Indicators of Success |
|---|---|
| Teaching time | Follows the rhythm of the brain with lecture segments of 15 to 20 minutes followed by 10 minutes in which the students do something with the learning (for secondary students), or for elementary students, in approximately 10-minute segments, followed by opportunities to work with the new learning |
| Lesson plans | Indicate opportunities for students to stand and move, to go on field trips, and to explore the environment |
| Lesson plans | Indicate a variety of visual tools are used |
| Student projects | Indicate choices that include visual, kinesthetic, and auditory learning |

ments for secondary and 7- to 10-minute segments for elementary students, with time for processing in between, will be a place where quality learning is possible.

Figure 2.3 shows common indicators of success for this teaching strategy.

# Strategies That Help Students Make Connections From Prior Learning and Experiences to New Learning and Across Disciplines

*Teachers should not assume that transfer will automatically occur after students acquire a sufficient base of information. Significant and efficient transfer occurs only if we teach to achieve it.*

—David Sousa (1995), *How the Brain Learns*

Sousa (1995) refers to the brain's process of making connections between old and new learning as transfer. The strength of this process is dependent on two factors. First, the effect of the past learning on the new learning and second, the degree to which the new learning will be useful in the future. When new information is introduced to working memory, a search is conducted in long-term memory for past learning that connects to the new learning. When those connections are made successfully, Sousa says that greater achievement is possible. He refers to this as positive transfer. Negative transfer occurs when past learning interferes with new learning. Sousa uses the example of learning to drive a standard shift car after driving only an automatic shift car in the past. The skill of leaving the left foot on the floor of the car for driving an automatic shift car can be a hindrance if transferred to the standard shift car where the left foot must be moved onto the clutch for shifting.

What if there are no prior experiences or knowledge of the subject to be taught? We have said that the brain is a seeker of connections. We have all had the experience of being in a room where something is being discussed about which we have no knowledge. There is confusion and frustration while we work to find a connection or hook for the new information. For some students this is a daily occurrence. What this means in the classroom is that we cannot

21

assume that students come to us with the structures already in place to learn new material. We must first establish what they know and understand and, where there are no previous connections, supply them for the student. John Bruer (1993) makes a strong case for the relevance of prior knowledge: "A good teacher will consciously capture attention and relate it to prior knowledge because how we understand and remember new material depends on what we already know. Our brains make sense of what we experience by actively connecting it with prior knowledge." Pyle and Andre (1986) echo these findings: "What a student acquires from instruction is determined as much by what the student already knows as by the nature of the instruction. Using previous knowledge to elaborate upon the presented information facilitates its transfer into long term memory." When the student relates new information to old information already in long-term memory, the student is more likely to learn and remember the new information. Prior to the introduction of new material, we must first find out if the prerequisite knowledge is there.

Sousa (1995) identifies four factors originally identified by Madeline Hunter that influence the rate and degree of retrieval. They include *similarity, critical attributes, association/context,* and *degree of original learning*. Let's look at the four factors and how classroom teachers might use them to help students make connections.

The first factor is *association*. Sousa defines association as events, actions, or feelings that are learned together so that the recall of one prompts the recall of the other. In my book *Strategies for Teaching Differently* (Walker, 1998), I refer to this part of the lesson as "personal connection" because it is the process of providing a hook or connection that makes the learning personal. Personal or association connection is based on the association of past experience, past knowledge, or, in the event that there are no past experiences, on the associations that we create. It is the process of going from the known to the unknown. This is probably the most common way that teachers help students bridge the new-learning gap. We want to find some experience or information that the student already has in long-term memory to which we can connect the new information. This is why teachers often refer back to previous lessons if the information to be studied requires the prerequisite of the information from the previous lesson. When there is no previous lesson from which to draw, we can create the hook with personal experiences the students may have had. If we can draw from personal experiences, especially those with emotional ties, we have a greater chance of making the new information relevant to the learner. As mentioned in Chapter 1, the brain ties itself to strong emotions. The amygdala, found in the forebrain, is responsible for encoding emotional messages and bonding them to the learning for long-term storage. Emotion is so strong in the brain that it takes priority over everything else. We are therefore more likely to remember something when we have an emotional tie to it. I often ask audiences to think back to the youngest age they can remember. The events they remember are usually either very happy or traumatic. Both are strong emotional ties. Emotions can also have a negative effect on making connections. Students who have always experienced problems with math will come to math class with negative transfer even before the lessons begin. When drawing on past experiences to which students may have emotional ties to introduce new information, the following examples given by Nancy Whisler and Judy Williams (1990) may be helpful: In elementary school, prior to reading "Earrings" by Judith Viorst, ask, "Have you ever wanted to do something that your parents said you could not because you weren't old enough?" In middle school, prior to a lesson on the Boston Tea Party, ask, "Have you ever encountered a rule that you felt was unfair to you in some way? Did you try to talk to someone about it? Did they listen?"

Personal or association connection is the piece that gives ownership to the learning process. Prior to a lesson on estimation, ask, "Have you ever seen those contests where you must guess how many jellybeans are in a jar?" By giving the problem personal application we create ownership. All of us are more interested in things to which we feel personal attachment: "What kind of strategy would you use to win the contest?" Prediction is another way we help create ownership of the learning by using students' natural curiosity to hook them into the learning. This is the marketing to which I referred earlier. We want to know about tomorrow's weather so we can plan accordingly, so we wait diligently during the news. Just before commercial break, the newscaster says, "Big changes coming in the weather, stay tuned after our commercial break for the details." They have us hooked so we will stay around for the details. This is a great technique to hook kids into reading and learning material that otherwise might not seem exciting. Fitzgerald (1996) gives these examples of using prediction to hook kids into the learning:

> A science teacher is introducing a unit on electro-magnetic radiation so he holds an electric razor up to an electro-magnetic radiation meter to set off the warning light. (An indication of radiation above the recommended level for human tissue.) A speech teacher shows clips from the Kennedy-Nixon debate and asks what skills or lack thereof will influence the outcome.

Elementary teachers often use this technique by showing pictures or giving information prior to reading a story to pique the kids' interest. A secondary teacher says, "In Romeo and Juliet there is going to be a major fight between two gangs tonight. What do you think will happen?" Sousa (1995) says that these hooks or connections should be given to students a day, even a week, before the learning to give them thinking time to get interested in the subject.

Personal or association connection is the link between previous knowledge and new knowledge: "Last week, we talked about slope and how it is used in the real world to figure the dimensions of handicap ramps. Today, we are going to measure handicap ramps around the building. Before we do that, let's review what the law says about the dimensions of these ramps and how we determine slope." Not only are we linking knowledge but we have also heightened the need to know with the fact that the students are going to do something with the information.

Figure 3.1 is an *association* tool that I use to help students make connections between old learning and experiences and new learning.

Before introducing a new unit, I ask my students to brainstorm ideas or information that they already know about the new subject. Those thoughts and information are written in the first circle. For example, for our unit on world hunger, I ask them to list everything they already know about world hunger in the inner circle. Then I ask them to look at the information that they have listed, and I ask them to place any information that would be related to transportation in the Category 1 circle, anything that would be considered to be related to politics in the Category 2 circle, anything that would be related to medical conditions in the Category 3 circle, and so on. By asking students not only to recall information, but to put it into categories, I am providing word associations early in the learning to help them retrieve information when they need it. This also provides the teacher with important information. What do students already know about this subject that doesn't need to be retaught, and what misinformation do they have that needs to be corrected up front before they place it in long-term memory? A word of caution on any technique to introduce a lesson: Be sure that information that is not correct is corrected immediately so that the incorrect information does not become a part of long-term memory. We tend to remember those things that are discussed in the first 20 minutes of class, so it is critical that we make the most of that time in getting important facts on the table correctly. After the students have made their lists and we have made a class master list from their information, I give them a lead-in or emotional hook to create interest. I might say, "In this country we produce enough food each year for every man, woman, and child in the world to have 2,200 calories each day, so why do we have world hunger?" By giving them an interesting tidbit of information about world hunger—that it is not a matter of food production, which most of them thought—I hook them into the learning. Then I lead them to ask questions. This approach is not unlike the evening news programs that give us a small amount of information just before commercial break to keep us watching. Then I ask, "So, what would you like to know about world hunger?" From the information that they provide, I make a "Want to know" list. During the unit on world hunger, we will refer back to this list often so that students can see that their questions and concerns are being answered. By doing this, I am giving them a *personal connection* or association to the learning.

Association or personal connection can also be the bridge between disciplines. There are many natural links between disciplines, and we need to point these out to students. We cannot assume that they will naturally get the relationship between the study of World War II in history and the study of John Hersey's novel *Hiroshima* in English class. In our restructured high

**FIGURE 3.1.** KWL Chart

| K(now) | W(ant to know) | L(earned) |
| --- | --- | --- |
| | | |

Categories: 1.

2.

3.

4.

5.

school we had a wedding to marry math to science and English to history. Teachers worked across disciplines to realign the curriculum so that those natural connections could take place at the same time. We did not change what we taught, just when we taught it. As we became more cognizant of what our colleagues were teaching, the benefits were transferred to our students. Departments made joint assignments so that instead of several fragmented projects, the projects moved across disciplines. Because students were working on fewer individual projects, they could present more complex, in-depth projects. In elementary school, we have a natural vehicle for doing this since the schedule allows the same teacher to teach across disciplines. As schools become more advanced in this technique and as student e-mail is introduced into classrooms, students will have opportunities to create projects that not only go across disciplines, but across grade levels as well.

The second factor affecting transfer is *similarity*. Sousa (1995) defines similarity as the process of transfer "generated by the similarity of the situation in which something is being learned and the situation to which that learning may transfer." Thus behavior in one environment tends to transfer to other environments that are similar. He uses the example of pilots who are trained in simulators and then transfer that experience to the actual plane.

In my book (Walker, 1998), I use similarity when students do not have exact prior knowledge or experience to connect to the new learning. In this instance, I relate the new information to something similar that they already understand personally. Jacoby (1991) uses a demonstration lesson on immigration that showcases this concept very well. Before beginning the unit, she asks, "What would have to happen in your life to cause you to pick up everything you can carry and move to a place where you know no one and a place about which you know very little?" Because students tend to give her the same kinds of answers, she then asks, "What would have to happen economically in this country to make you leave? In the religious arena? Politically? Medically?" That way, when she gets around to talking about why people get in leaky boats and risk their lives to emigrate, students have a connection for understanding.

The third factor that affects transfer is *critical attributes*. Sousa (1995) identifies critical attributes as "characteristics that make one idea unique from all others." *Unique* is the key word here, since it is important that students identify how things are different so that retrieval will be easier. Sousa says that long-term memory files new information into a network with similar information, but when it retrieves it, memory looks for differences so that the right piece of information is retrieved. He uses the example that we recognize our best friend not by the attributes that make him like everyone else, but by features that make him unique. We have all had the experience of looking for someone in a crowd. For a moment, everyone looks alike; they all have faces, bodies, and hair. The way we find the person we are seeking is in looking for features unique to that person, such as black hair, tall body, and sharp chin.

**FIGURE 3.2.** Indicators of a Classroom in Which Curriculum Facilitates Transfer From Prior Learning Experiences to New Learning and Across Disciplines

| Assessment Tools | Indicators of Success |
|---|---|
| Lesson plans | Indicate that students are provided opportunities to create connections to the new learning at the beginning of new lessons or units. Where prior knowledge and experience do not exist, the teacher provides that information before going to the new material. |

Since the brain already has stored patterns and structures from previous learning and experiences, teachers build on those patterns for similar information that is new. This technique makes use of the brain's search for patterns for understanding. Patterns might be categories such as those given in the example on immigration or patterns such as those in mnemonic devices. Graphic models are great tools to help visual students create attributes. Use mindmaps or organization tables with key concepts to help students form patterns for the new learnings. Since 80% of the learners in the classroom learn either visually or kinesthetically (Jenson, 1998), it is important to include visual models to help connect the learning.

The fourth factor that influences transfer is *context and degree of original learning.* Sousa (1995) says that when the original learning was well learned and accurate, new learning will be more powerful. This factor is a great argument for teaching a concept for mastery, not just to cover the subject. Many teachers are frustrated by the amount of material that is required by state, national, or local policies without regard to whether the students actually learn it. We can only hope that as brain research is understood, schools will take another look at not only how information is taught, but the time frame in which it is taught.

**In conclusion:** Eric Jenson (1998) says, "The brain thrives on meaning, not random information."

We should not assume that students come to us with the necessary structures in place to make the necessary connections to new information and across disciplines. We must first find out what they know, what misinformation they have about the subject, and, where no structures exist, create structures for the new information. When we do this, we help students "get it" from the very beginning. Although it takes some class time to do this, it may very well save time in the long run because reteaching will not be needed to the degree that it would be without it.

Figure 3.2 shows indicators of success with this technique.

# Teaching for Long-Term Memory Is a Primary Goal

# 4

*H*ave you ever crammed for a test, aced the test, and then 2 weeks later encountered a question from the test and said, "What in the world is that?" We have all had the experience of frustration from teaching a great lesson only to find out weeks later that the students remember very little of what was taught. Schools have often emphasized the fact that students must learn material for "the test" rather than learning because it has relevance to student needs beyond "the test." While the brain is willing to put information into short-term memory for a short-term goal, it needs more incentive for remembering for the long term.

Chapter 2 discussed the three modalities through which we receive incoming information. They include visual, which is stored in the occipital lobe at the back of the brain; auditory, which is processed and stored in the temporal lobes on the sides of the brain near the ears; and kinesthetic, which is stored at the top of the brain in the motor cortex and later in the cerebellum. Once the information enters the brain through the various modalities, it is held in the association cortex until it is either tossed out, sent to working memory, or sent back to long-term memory (Springer, 1999). Once new learning has been registered through the perceptual or sensory register in the brain stem, it moves to temporary memory, which is made up of short-term memory which is an extension of the perceptual register, and working memory where processing occurs (Sousa, 1995). Short-term memory holds information for only about 30 seconds while it decides whether to toss it or move it along. Sousa uses the example of looking up a phone number and retaining it only long enough to call the number. If the number is needed later, it will have to be looked up in the telephone directory again. Because the number was not perceived to be important enough to be put into long-term memory, the brain tossed it after the number was called.

Working memory is the place where information is processed. At this point, the information has our attention while we mull it over. Working memory can handle only a few chunks of information at one time. Sousa says that pre-school infants deal with only two items of information at once, pre-adolescents deal with three to seven items with an average of five. From adolescence through adulthood, seven to nine chunks are handled at one time with seven being the average (Sousa, 1995). Jenson (1998) uses a similar guide. He says that infants hold about one item of information in working memory at one time, with the number increasing by one every other year of life to adolescence where seven to nine items are held in working memory. There is a difference of opinion on how long information remains in working memory before being tossed out or sent to long-term memory, but it seems to be about 5 to 10 minutes for pre-adolescent children and 10 to 20 minutes for adolescents and adults. Sousa says that after 20 minutes, if something is not done with it, the information will probably be dropped from working memory.

If the learner is ever to recall this information in the future, it must be stored in long-term memory. The brain holds information in working memory while it decides whether to send it on to long-term memory. In order to understand long-term memory, we must look at the brain's storage system. There are at least five memory pathways in the brain. I use the analogy of a five-drawer file cabinet that assists with retrieval in the brain.

Each drawer represents a different storage system. The systems are *semantic*, which holds information from words; *episodic*, which deals with locations; *procedural*, which deals with processes; *automatic*, which deals with conditioned response; and *emotional*, which takes precedence over all other types of memory (Jenson, 1998). Let's look at each of these drawers in our memory file cabinet individually.

*Semantic memory* holds the information that was learned from words. New information enters through the brain stem and passes through the thalamus to the hippocampus where a search is conducted for matching information. If a connection is made, the information will go to working memory (Jenson, 1998).

Two hooks or attachments are important in ensuring that the brain stores the information in long-term memory. These three hooks boost the process.

The first hook for semantic memory is relevance or meaning. The question becomes, "What does this have to do with the world in which I live?" We have all had students who ask, "When are we ever going to use this?" Students ask not to drive us crazy, but because they really need to know in order to make the learning meaningful. Several years ago I attended one of William Glasser's workshops. Glasser said that he could teach anyone anything as long as he could make it relevant. He said that after all, very young children learn one of the hardest things to learn—they learn a language—and no one stands in front of them with flash cards. They learn it because it is relevant to their world. If we can give the information relevance in the classroom,

**FIGURE 4.1.** The Brain's Retrieval System

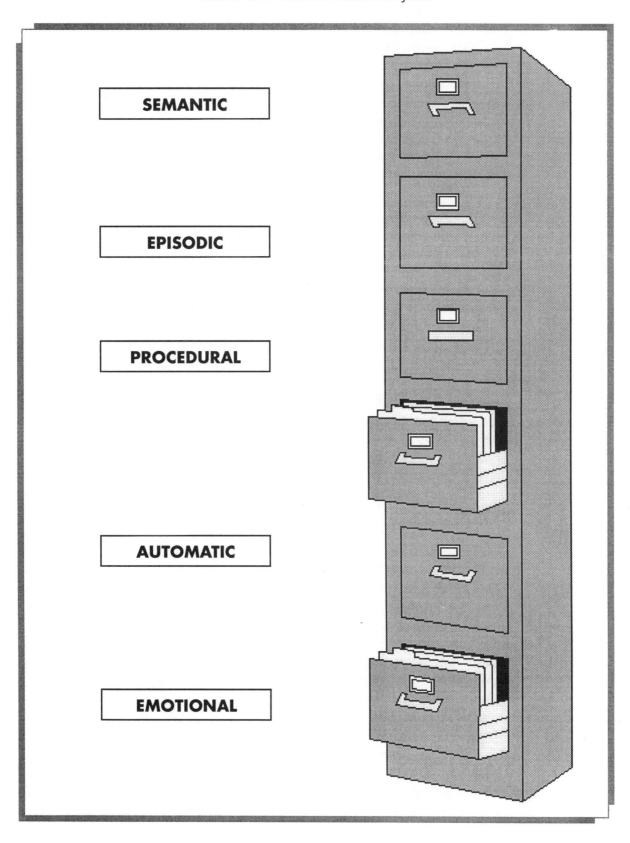

there is a good chance that it will be remembered. Keefe (1997) says we can create meaning by modeling, by giving examples from experience, and through artificial meaning such as mnemonic devices.

The second hook for semantic memory is patterns created by prior knowledge or experience. Sousa (1995) calls this "making sense" of the information. Is there already a pattern in place into which the new information can fit? Do I have prior knowledge or prior experience with which to hook onto the new information? Students will be able to learn and remember statistics more easily if they have a prior knowledge of algebra. Jenson (1995) cites the work of Nummela Caine, which concludes that, "The ability to make meaningful sense out of countless bits of data is critical to understanding and motivation." Jenson suggests that prior to the learning we create a global overview, give oral previews, or post mindmaps to help form the patterns for the instruction. During the learning, allow students to discuss the topic and to create models, mindmaps, or pictures. After finishing a topic, give the learners the opportunity to evaluate it, discuss relevance, or demonstrate patterning with models, plays, or teachings. For example, Pat Jacoby (1991) introduces a unit on immigration by asking students what would cause them to leave this country. Next, she asks what would have to happen in this country politically for them to leave. Economically? In the religious arena? By doing that, she provides a hook or pattern for the learning that is about to take place. When students get around to the economic, religious, and political reasons why people emigrate, they have prior learning to create a hook for the new learning. During the lesson, provide opportunities for students to use the information in visuals such as mindmaps or through written diagrams. Jenson (1998) says that the semantic memory pathway requires repetition of the learning and needs to be stimulated by associations, comparisons, and similarities. The immigration example makes use of associations in a concrete way.

Of the two hooks, relevance and patterns, Sousa (1995) says the most important is relevance. He goes on to say that most classrooms spend the majority of lesson time on making sense of the new information and little time on giving it relevance. By shifting the emphasis to relevance, students would more likely retain the learning at a higher rate.

The second memory drawer in our file cabinet is *episodic*. Episodic memory has to do with where we were when we learned something. Springer (1999) uses the example of tending to remember where we were at the time of a traumatic event such as the assassination of John Kennedy. According to her, students who learn information in one room and are tested in another tend to underperform. This has tremendous implications for giving standardized tests to students in the room in which they prepared for the test.

Springer (1999) also talks about the invisible information within a room. For example, if a bulletin board in a room has information about the multiplication tables and the information is taken down while students take a test on multiplication, students tend to look at the blank bulletin board to help recall facts. Kay Toliver (1995), the outstanding teacher who has had so much success with teaching the at-risk children of Harlem, uses props to help students with learning. For a math lesson on multiplication, she came to class with placards across the front and back of her torso that were a replica of a box of raisins. Her students worked with multiplication using raisins. What a great tool to help students when it comes time for recall on multiplication facts! Springer (1999) uses fact sheets printed on different colors of paper, depending on the subject of the fact sheets. When students are having trouble with recall, she mentions the color of the paper that contained the facts.

One example of the way in which episodic memory is used might be that of watching television when the commercial for some type of medication comes on. That reminds us that we need to call the pharmacy to renew a prescription. We get up to go to the bedroom to make the call. On the way, a family member asks a question that we answer but, by the time we get to the bedroom, we can't remember why we are there. We go back to the couch in front of the television and at the next commercial we suddenly remember why we went to the bedroom. Our memory was triggered by the suggestion from the television and then by the place we were sitting when we received the cue. Once we are distracted we lose the cue, but sitting back on the couch helps to re-cue us to go call the pharmacy.

The third drawer of our memory file cabinet is for *procedural* memory. Procedural memory is actually stored in the cerebellum, which is responsible for muscle coordination (Sousa, 1995). Processes such as driving a car are stored in this part of the brain. Rehearsal plays an important part in this memory. For example, I will not be able to remember how to drive a car unless I have practiced the process. If we want students to perform an operation easily, we must have them rehearse or perform the material often enough that it becomes procedural. One of Steven Covey's (1989) rules is called the 28-day rule. Basically, the rule says that if you repeat a behavior for 28 days, it becomes internalized. Often used in changing behaviors, this rule draws on procedural memory to change negative thinking into positive by repetition. Jenson (1998) says that we enhance procedural memory through hands-on activities, manipulatives, role play, and physical skills.

The fourth drawer of the memory file cabinet is *automatic or conditioned response*. Automatic memory is triggered by stimuli. Any learning that has become automatic is stored in this drawer. For example, the ability to read is found in this drawer, but the ability to understand the reading is not. Other memory drawers, such as semantic, deal with meaning. The alphabet, multiplication tables, and so on, can also be found in the automatic drawer. When the information is tedious or when it is not used often, such as vocabulary words that are not used in everyday conversation, mnemonic devices can act as triggers. Jenson (1998) says that if we can weave a story around the information, it is more likely that students will remember. I often use an example of this with audiences. I tell them that I am going to teach them a vocabulary word in such a way that they will remember it for the rest of their lives. The word I teach is *ingratiate.* I tell the following story:

In our town we have a woman named Barbara who is a single lady. She would like to get married but has not been successful as yet. She went to the bookstore and bought some of those self-help books on marriage, such as *How to Marry a Millionaire,* because she has decided that when she gets married, it will be to someone who has money. In our town is a bachelor named Bill who just happens to be a millionaire. He is a confirmed bachelor and is not interested in getting married. For some reason, Barbara has decided that he is the one. She has tried everything to get him to ask her out, but without success. Finally, she decided to take matters into her own hands and asked him to dinner at her house. Now, he is a bachelor and he doesn't get a home-cooked meal very often, so he decided he could put up with going out for one night for a home-cooked meal. In preparation for the big date, Barbara went shopping and bought a new red dress and shoes. On the night of the date, she dressed in her new outfit; as a matter of fact she looked great. When Bill rang the doorbell, Barbara answered the door. She had an experience that many of us have had where the other person's face falls and you know something is wrong. Barbara asked what was wrong and Bill reluctantly told her that he just didn't care for red dresses. Barbara assured him that was not a problem and invited him into the living room to wait while she changed her dress. Her second favorite dress was a blue dress, so she put it on and returned to the living room. Bill said the dress didn't do anything for her. She said that was not a problem, she would change. She put on a green dress, but he thought it didn't go with her eyes; she put on a black dress, but it reminded him of his poor mother's funeral; and she put on a purple dress but he didn't care for the fabric. Finally, the only dress that she had left in her closet was an old gray dress that she hardly wore, but it was the only thing left so she put it on and returned to the living room. Bill exclaimed that he loved it, that he had always loved a woman in gray. While they were having dinner, Bill got to thinking that any woman who would go to such great lengths to please him might make a good wife, after all, and he began thinking of marriage. The moral of the story is that any time you know someone who goes to great lengths to please another person, you can remember my friend Barbara and "in gray she ate," and you will remember the meaning of the word *ingratiate.*

I was doing a workshop in California and a man in my audience told me that he uses this tool to help teach his students the parts of the body in his anatomy class. He has made up an elaborate story about a man who gets caught in a snow bank, and through the story he uses the names of the parts of the body to tell the story. For example, the man who tries to pull the car out of the snow is the pullman, he is doing the most work because he is pulling instead of pushing. He is like the pulmonary artery. He said that what was once difficult for students to remember has now become easy through this technique.

The fifth drawer of the memory file cabinet is the most powerful of all the memory drawers, *emotion*. The brain tends to remember those things to which it has an emotional attachment. Eric Jenson (1995) says, "The stronger the emotion, the more the meaning. Emotional experiences 'code' our learning as important." Think back to the youngest age you can remember. If you are like most of us, your earliest remembrance is probably either very happy or traumatic in some way. That is because the brain remembers vivid emotional experiences. My earliest remembrance was when I was 4 years old. I thought it would be fun to hide from my parents, so I went outside and hid in a corner of our house. It was all fun until I saw my parents go by looking for me, and they were not having fun—they were very upset. I later learned that they had the whole neighborhood out looking for me. Jenson (1995) says we tend to remember our highest highs and our lowest lows. "This applies across all areas of life: the best and the worst vacations, meals, dates, jobs, weather and so on." Emotions can and do influence retention. Jenson (1995) goes on to say,

> Make a purposeful strategy to engage positive emotions within the learner. Without it, the learner may not code the material learned as important. Long, continuous lectures and predictable lessons are the least likely to be remembered. Utilize the following: enthusiasm, drama, role-playing, quiz shows, music, debates, larger projects, guest speakers, creative controversy, adventures, impactful rituals and celebrations.

**In conclusion:** In a classroom in which a conscious effort is being made to ensure that students are putting the information into long-term memory and will be able to retrieve it when needed, teachers will provide tools to help facilitate the process. Emotion, relevance, and concrete models that assist students to move random facts to a concrete form will be an ongoing part of the teaching process. Teachers will employ techniques that pique student interest and that motivate students to know more. Lessons will be dynamic, high interest, and will employ emotion where appropriate. Students will see the application to real life so that they "buy into" the learning from the start. The teacher, as role model, will demonstrate a love for learning that will translate to students. In this environment, students and learning will thrive.

**FIGURE 4.2.** Indicators of a Classroom in Which
Teaching for Long-Term Memory Is a Primary Goal

| Assessment Tools | Indicators of Success |
| --- | --- |
| Lesson plans | Indicate that teachers employ techniques to pique student interest in the learning |
| Lesson plans and observations | Indicate that lessons are dynamic, of high interest, and presented in such a way that students are actively involved |
| Students' tasks and projects | Indicate use of emotion, relevance, and high-interest materials |
| Student assessment | Includes opportunities for reflection and self-assessment |

Figure 4.2 shows the indicators of success for the strategies discussed in this chapter.

# Integrating Higher-Level Thinking Skills Into Learning 5

*Regrettably, teachers are more likely to increase difficulty rather than complexity, when attempting to raise student thinking.*

—David Sousa (1997), *How the Brain Learns: New Insights Into the Teaching/Learning Process*

Students deserve to be given meaningful, challenging work. It is an insult to give students mounds of dittos or meaningless busy work to fill up time. "Time on task" is important only if the task is meaningful. William Glasser, in an interview in *Phi Delta Kappan,* stated,

> If half of all students are not working because they perceive that school will not satisfy their needs, we have to attend to the fact that a major institution in our society—perhaps the one on which we spend the most money—follows a theory that does not address itself to the needs of more than half of its clients. (cited in Gough, 1993)

Sousa (1995) warns that there is a significant difference between complexity and difficulty. Complexity refers to the thought processes that the brain uses to deal with information. Each level of Bloom's Taxonomy (Bloom, 1976) represents a different level of complexity. Difficulty, however, refers to the amount of effort expended within a level of complexity. A learner might expend a great deal of energy on difficulty while working at a low level of complexity. Sousa gives the example of requiring a student to name the states and their capitals in order of their admission to the Union. This example takes place on the lowest level of Bloom's, the knowledge level, but requires some effort on the part of the student. Knowledge is considered to be low level because the student does not even need to understand the information in order to process the question, he merely needs to be able to provide facts from a book. While there is certainly nothing wrong with this assignment, students who are never allowed to go beyond this level, or who expend so much effort at the low levels that they do not have time for the higher levels of thought, are robbed of the opportunity to grow mentally. Teachers mistakenly think that slower students cannot work in the higher levels of the taxonomy, although studies by Bloom (1976) show that the opposite is true. When these students are given only the critical attributes of the learning, without extraneous information to sort, they are able to perform at a more complex level.

Sousa (1995) concludes that teachers can get slower students to be successful at the higher levels of Bloom's Taxonomy if they review the curriculum and remove extraneous information and topics of least importance, and provide time for practice at the higher levels.

Newmann and Wehlage (1993) suggest that we "Ask to what extent does the given activity engage students in using their minds well." Learning in this new century will be less about reciting names, dates, and places and more about critical thinking applications such as problem solving, synthesis, creativity, analysis, and evaluation. Computers can store the names, dates, and places; computers cannot perform the critical analyses and interpersonal skills necessary to solve complex problems. Newmann and Wehlage (1993) define lower-order thinking (LOT) as that which "occurs when students are asked to receive or recite factual information or to employ rules and algorithms through repetitive routines." They define higher-order thinking (HOT) as thinking that "requires students to manipulate information and ideas in ways that transform their meaning and implications, such as when students combine facts and ideas in order to synthesize, generalize, explain, hypothesize or arrive at some conclusion or interpretation."

There are three basic reasons for using higher-order thinking in the daily instruction of students. They are the need for *information literacy,* the need for *quality processes,* and the need for *quality products.* These three reasons involve processes that require critical and creative thought, which require students to look at information frontward, backward, and in ways never viewed before.

First, higher-order thinking is a basic part of being information literate. Resnick and Resnick (1997) identify literacy as rational thinking. This involves the ability to analyze information, extrapolate key points, generate a hypothesis, draw conclusions, and find viable solutions. With the influx of technology and research using the Internet, knowing the difference between primary and secondary sources has become exceedingly important. If students are to become an essential part of the information age, they must be given the tools to know how to evaluate material and to determine how to use it, not only for themselves but for the benefit of others as well. Higher-order thinking skills, such as critical thinking, creative thinking, and problem solving, are important if students are to be successful. Figure 5.1 depicts the categories of critical and creative thinking along with problem solving and some of their components.

**FIGURE 5.1.** Using Higher-Level Thinking Skills

I. Critical Thinking is the ability to analyze, to create and use objective criteria, and to evaluate data. Critical thinking includes the following:

A. Inductive Thinking Skills

- ► Cause and effect
- ► Open-ended problems
- ► Analogy
- ► Making inferences
- ► Identifying relevance
- ► Relationships
- ► Problem solving

B. Deductive Thinking Skills

- ► Using logic
- ► Understanding contradiction
- ► Syllogisms
- ► Spatial problems

C. Evaluative Thinking Skills

- ► Fact and opinion
- ► Credibility of a source
- ► Identifying central issues and problems
- ► Recognizing underlying assumptions
- ► Detecting bias, stereotypes, cliches
- ► Evaluating hypotheses
- ► Classifying data
- ► Predicting consequences
- ► Sequencing
- ► Decision-making skills
- ► Recognizing propaganda
- ► Similarities and differences
- ► Evaluating arguments

*(Continued)*

**FIGURE 5.1.** Continued

II. Creative thinking is the ability to use complex thinking structures to produce new and original ideas. Creative thinking includes the following tools:

- ▶ Attributes
- ▶ Fluency
- ▶ Flexibility
- ▶ Originality
- ▶ Elaboration
- ▶ Synthesis

III. Problem solving is the ability to utilize complex thinking to solve real problems. The steps may include:

- ▶ Identifying the problem
- ▶ Analyzing the problem
- ▶ Formulating a hypothesis
- ▶ Formulating appropriate questions
- ▶ Generating ideas
- ▶ Developing alternative solutions
- ▶ Determining the best solution
- ▶ Applying the solution
- ▶ Monitoring and evaluating the solution
- ▶ Drawing conclusions

Critical thinking is the ability to think at a complex level and to use analysis and evaluation processes. Critical thinking involves inductive thinking skills such as recognizing relationships, analyzing open-ended problems, determining cause and effect, making inferences, and extrapolating relevant data. Deductive thinking skills include solving spatial problems, logic, syllogisms, and distinguishing fact from opinion. Other critical-thinking skills include detecting bias, evaluating, comparing and contrasting, and the ability to distinguish between fact and opinion.

Creative thinking is complex thinking that produces new and original ideas. Paul Torrence (1966) is considered by many to be the father of creative thinking. He developed a model around four attributes:

1. Fluency: the ability to generate many ideas. An example would be to ask students to brainstorm what they know about world hunger.

2. Flexibility: the ability to generate many different ideas. An example would be to ask students to brainstorm what they know about world hunger in regard to medical aspects, economic aspects, political aspects, and so on.

3. Originality: the ability to generate unique ideas.

4. Elaboration: the ability to generate many details.

Problem solving uses sequential skills to solve complex problems and incorporates the ability to see and analyze underlying causes.

Second, these skills are necessary because students must have higher-order thinking skills in order to perform quality processes. O'Tuel and Bullard (1993) say "process is as important as product in education. Note that the words 'as important' not 'more important than' were used. This is because students need an information base upon which to build." We all tend to be creative when we are children, but sometimes in elementary school that creativity takes a nose dive. Major corporations have put megabucks into retraining their people to be creative. Creativity is essential in a world where change is happening so quickly. If business, industry, education, or any other institution is to survive and remain marketable, it must involve the processes of creative and critical thinking. Joel Barker (1992), in his book *Future Edge*, says that the element that will make our students marketable in this new century is not quality—that will be the minimum expectation—it is creativity.

Curriculum must include opportunities for students to utilize higher-order thinking skills such as the ability to use both convergent and divergent processes, to think critically, and to investigate real-world solutions to complex problems.

Newmann and Wehlage (1993) say, "Knowledge is thin or superficial when it does not deal with significant concepts of a topic or discipline—for example when students have a trivial understanding of important concepts or when they have only a surface acquaintance with their meaning." The reason for this is usually an attempt to cover quantities of information.

> Knowledge is deep or thick when it concerns the central ideas of a topic or discipline. For students, knowledge is deep when they make clear distinctions, develop arguments, solve problems, construct explanations, and otherwise work with relatively complex understanding. Depth is produced, in part, by covering fewer topics in systematic and connected ways. (Newmann & Wehlage, 1993)

Third, higher-order thinking leads students to create quality products. How many of us have assigned independent studies to classes only to receive finished products that are far less than our expectations. Time is too precious a commodity in schools to waste in producing finished products that are low

**FIGURE 5.2.** A Formula for Student Projects

| Bloom's Level | Verb | Process | Product |
|---|---|---|---|
|  |  |  |  |

level and below the abilities of our students. Finished products should reflect the higher-order thinking skills of quality processes. At the highest level, the products should benefit not only the student, but others as well. If we use the rationale of Bloom's Taxonomy, for example, it is possible to provide students with high-quality expectations for finished products by providing clear parameters for the finished product. Teachers must set parameters that ensure quality, then must teach the process skills, and must set benchmarks so that there are no surprises when the finished product is turned in. Figure 5.2 shows a process for assigning student projects.

Simply put, the levels of Bloom's Taxonomy include

1. Knowledge level: to know something and be able to recite it back. Verbs that indicate assignments at this level include *list, outline, recall, locate,* and *describe.*

2. Comprehension: to understand something and to be able to explain it. Verbs that indicate assignments at this level include *interpret, demonstrate, explain,* and *infer.*

3. Application: the ability to use information and ideas. Verbs that indicate assignments at this level include *apply, classify, organize, solve,* and *use.*

4. Synthesis: the ability to take something apart and put it back together in new and unusual ways. Verbs that indicate assignments at this level include *combine, construct, generate,* and *reorganize.*

5. Analysis: the ability to break something down into manageable parts. Words that indicate assignments at this level include *differentiate, diagram, infer, simplify,* and *syllogism.*

6. Evaluation: the ability to judge something. Verbs that indicate assignments at this level include *appraise, determine, evaluate, weigh,* and *rank.*

**FIGURE 5.3.** Examples of Formulas for Student Projects

| Bloom's Level | Verb | Process | Product |
|---|---|---|---|
| Knowledge | list | the freedoms included in the Bill of Rights | as a newspaper ad to encourage patriotism |
| Comprehension | explain | slope to your class | in such a way that a student new to class would understand |
| Application | draw | illustrate how to identify and classify parallelograms | flowchart |
| Analysis | analyze | the organizational structure of two works of art from the Renaissance period | compare and contrast chart |
| Synthesis | create | using the elements of short story writing and information relating to compromises, property, and the aftermath | an original short story about the talks at Yalta |
| Evaluation | judge | the underlying reasons for World War II | a rank order chart with narrative |

7. Remember, Bloom's does not get more difficult as we move up the taxonomy—we can add difficulty at any level—it becomes more complex.

To use the taxonomy, a teacher would determine the level or levels of Bloom's in which the product would fall, use the appropriate verb to distinguish the Bloom's level, identify a process to produce the product, and then identify an appropriate product. Students should be given choices of products. This follows the philosophy of constructivist thinking, which holds that we learn based on schema or patterns already established and that we interpret new stimulus and information based on that schema. O'Tuel and Bullard (1993) give the example of a large dog in a yard. One person might approach the dog with no fear because he has a similar dog at home, while another might hide behind a tree because of a negative experience with another dog. Because we do react differently to new information, and because we want to encourage creativity, students should be given some choices in the way learning is approached. If we want quality, however, we must set the parameters.

The teacher might provide a list of possibilities from which students choose their projects. The value of the projects might differ according to the level of difficulty. See Figure 5.3 for examples.

**FIGURE 5.4.** Indicators of a Classroom in Which Higher-Level Thinking Skills
Are Integrated Into the Lesson

| Assessment Tools | Indicators of Success |
| --- | --- |
| Student products | Indicate that critical-thinking skills, creative-thinking skills, and problem-solving skills are encouraged and rewarded |
| Student products and assessments | Are at the analysis level and above |
| Lesson plans | Indicate inductive thinking skills such as cause and effect |
| Lesson plans | Indicate deductive thinking skills such as logic and syllogisms |
| Student products | Indicate an understanding of the vocabulary of higher-order thinking skills |
| Student products | Indicate that students can perform the steps of complex problem solving |

**In conclusion:** When higher-order thinking skills are a part of the learning, students use more complex thinking processes. Critical thinking, creative thinking, and problem solving should be encouraged and rewarded. The teacher should filter the material to be studied so that low-level and extraneous information are kept at a minimum to allow time for processing more complex skills. To the extent possible, student products and assessments should be at the analysis level or above. Inductive thinking skills such as cause-and-effect and making inferences should be a part of the lesson plans, and students should be provided opportunities to use deductive thinking skills such as logic and syllogistic thinking. All students should have the opportunity to work at higher levels, not just students identified as fast learners. When we do this, we raise the floor of achievement, making our way to raising the roof.

Figure 5.4 shows the indicators that will be present when higher-order thinking skills are a part of the learning.

# Collaborative Learning Is an Integral Part of the Classroom

*[H]igh schools continue to go about their business in ways that sometimes bear startling resemblance to the flawed practices of the past. Students pursue their education largely in traditional classroom settings, taught by teachers who stand before row upon row of desks. Mostly, these teachers lecture at students, whose main participation in class is limited to terse answers to fact-seeking questions.*

—National Association of Secondary School Principals (1996), *Breaking Ranks*

Collaboration is more than just working together in groups; it is the whole communication process in the classroom. How does the teacher communicate with students in regard to the information to be learned, and how is it assessed? How do students communicate with the teacher and with each other? What is the role of the parent? Is the communication one way, two way, or multiple? Is it in the form of written, oral, tactile, computer-generated or communication?

In the studies reported by Diamond (1988) in which rats were placed in environments enriched with rat toys and compared with rats placed in impoverished environments with no rat toys, it was found that rats with rat toys had more dendritic branches than those without rat toys. What is significant for the need for collaboration is another phase of her study. In this experiment, one rat was placed in a cage with rat toys (enriched environment) and another rat was placed in a cage alone, without rat toys (impoverished environment). A control group of three rats was placed in a larger cage without rat toys. Although the single rat with rat toys grew more dendritic branches than the single rat with no rat toys, the rats that grew the most dendritic branches were the three rats placed together, even though they did not have rat toys.

This would suggest that we learn more in environments where we are with others.

To be successful in the job market, students must be able to articulate what they know and to listen to the ideas and opinions of others. Students practice cooperative and collaborative learning strategies to help solidify what they have learned and to practice the learning so that when it is time for individual assessment, the learning is in long-term memory. Sizer (cited in O'Neil, 1995) says,

> The real world demands collaboration, the collective solving of problems . . . learning to get along, to function effectively in a group is essential. Evidence and experience also strongly suggest that an individual's personal learning is enhanced by collaborative effort. The act of sharing ideas, of having to put one's own views clearly to others, of finding defensible compromises and conclusions, is in itself educative.

How can we ever expect students to learn the higher-level social task of criticizing ideas, not people, if they have not learned the basic task of collaborating effectively with others?

The Secretary's Commission on Achieving Necessary Skills (SCANS) report (U.S. Department of Labor, 1991) was an eye opener at the time it was released because it said that while it is important for students to know reading, mathematics, and writing skills, one of the most important marketable skills that we can give students is the ability to work with other people. That information should have been no surprise since we have known for years that the primary reason why people lose jobs is not incompetence but the inability to get along with others. Students need classroom opportunities to work with everyone else in the classroom at some point in time. Even very young children need social skills. It is one thing to know information; it is another to be able to explain that information to someone else. Add to that the ability to do quality problem solving with small groups and you have a winning combination. When we were working on research for our restructured school, one of our consultants visited with members of business and industry to ask firsthand what the important skills were that we should be teaching students. The answer was overwhelming that we should be teaching social and collaborative skills. One oil company said that when prospective employees come in for an interview, the company brings them in small groups to the office. There they are given a problem to solve. They are given a choice; they can work together on the solution or they can work in cubicles to solve the problem alone. What the prospective employees do not know is that if they choose to work alone, they will not be called back for a second interview. The Association of Supervision and Curriculum Development said in their 1999 yearbook, "The process of learning has passed from simple self-organization to collaborative, interpersonal, social problem-solving activity dependent on conversation, practical, meaningful involvement, and real world experience and application."

Four primary communications are important to making collaborative learning significant in the classroom. First, *communication between the teacher and students* is crucial. In Chapter 1, the significance of classroom environment and the power of a positive climate was presented. The teacher sets the tone for the classroom through verbal and non-verbal communication. Not only is what is said to students important, but the tone and body movements as well. Jenson (1998) says that high stress and threat in the classroom impair brain cells. He goes on to say, "Threat also changes the body's chemistry and impacts learning." If students are made to believe that no matter what they do, they cannot be successful in the classroom, threat exists. In Chapter 1, evidence was presented that the success of our students was dramatically raised just by saying to them that we would not let them fail and then backing that up with actions. Jenson (1998) provides these additional examples of threat in the classroom:

1. Anything that embarrasses students

2. Unrealistic deadlines

3. A student's inability to speak a language

4. Uncomfortable classroom cultures

5. A bully in the hallway

6. Inappropriate learning styles

7. Out-of-class factors such as a fight with family members

8. Threat of being sent to the principal

When threat exists, the brain operates in survival mode and while we can learn in that mode, we do so at the expense of higher-order thinking.

Once a positive climate has been established, the teacher must communicate expectations verbally and in writing. Why both? Eighty percent of the students in the classroom do not learn auditorily. Expectations include classroom rules as well as learning expectations. Prior to any assignment in which students will be assessed, they should be told verbally and in writing what they have to do to be successful—and that should be followed to the letter. When we tell students in advance what it takes to be successful, we take away the "gotchas." There are no surprises—students know in advance how they will be assessed, whether through a rubric or through some other written communication. These rubrics should be specific. When we do this, we help level the playing field so that everyone starts with the same opportunity for success.

**FIGURE 6.1.** Ticket Out the Door

THREE THINGS I HAVE LEARNED ARE

1. _____

_____

2. _____

_____

3. _____

_____

ONE THING I DO NOT UNDERSTAND IS

_____

_____

_____

Teachers must also set benchmarks, which include frequent intervals to check for student understanding. These should be interspersed within the class day or class period. Sousa (1995) says assessment for a grade should not come until 24 hours after learning because we cannot be sure that the information is in long-term memory until at least that amount of time has passed. Benchmarks, however, refer to making sure the students understand—not to assessment for grades.

Effective communication between students and teacher also requires cruise control. As a teacher, I cruise the room while my students are working so that I know on an ongoing basis who is off-task, who doesn't understand, and who is in danger of failing. When one of these factors is present, I can intervene immediately. Another tool for doing this is a tool I call "Ticket Out the Door." In my book (Walker, 1998) I provide examples of this technique. Basically, in order to get out the door when the bell rings, students must give me a ticket that has assigned questions. An example of a blank ticket out the door is shown in Figure 6.1.

For very young students, I use faces—happy face, sad face, and neutral face. Students give me a face that signals how they feel about the day. This is a non-threatening way for students to let me know if all is not going well and a tool for early intervention before it is too late.

Lastly, the teacher must begin to take on the role of coach, leader, or guide in the classroom to stir the students by dynamic, interesting presentations of the learning that allow students to participate actively. The teacher cannot continue to be the lecturer with the students as passive listeners. Students today come from a sound-byte world that constantly bombards the senses. They will not, cannot, sit all day as passive listeners. Jenson (1998) says, "Today's teachers must think of themselves as catalyst for learning, not a live, breathing textbook. Schools simply must have greater roles, like creating motivated, thinking, responsible, and productive citizens for the next century."

The second necessary communication link is *student-to-student communication.* Jenson (1998) says,

> Our brain cannot be good at everything, therefore, it selects over time that which will ensure its survival. As a species, the human brain has evolved to use language as our primary means for communication. This may partly explain why groups, teams and cooperative learning benefit our understanding and application of new concepts; group work requires us to communicate with each other. Through this process, learning seems to be enhanced.

We learn best when we teach something to someone else. As a teacher, when did you know your subject best—probably when you taught it to someone else. We need to make use of this powerful teaching technique by giving students opportunities to tell about the learning.

Students also need the opportunity to work with other people—not just their best friends. Social skills, group interaction skills, conversation skills, and group problem-solving skills are some of the highest-level skills we can give to our students. These skills may have more to do with their success in life than the academic skills we give them. They certainly have a great deal to do with their finding satisfying and rewarding relationships—both personal and collegial. For teachers who have not attempted group activities in the past but are convinced it is worth trying, I offer the following guidelines:

1. Start small—begin by letting students work in pairs for a short amount of time. The ideal time to use this would be after presenting information for 15 to 20 minutes, during the 10 minutes of down time. Have students discuss what has been said, formulate questions about the new material, or use the information in some way. Not only does this produce social skills, but it also helps solidify the new learning.

2. The first few times that students are put into small groups, use familiar material. A unit you have never taught before is not a good time to try group work for the first time.

3. Make sure that any assigned group work is meaningful. Students know when it is busy work and will react accordingly.

4. Time all activities and stick to the time schedule. Allow only enough time for the groups to do the work effectively—push the envelope a little. If you tell students they have 8 minutes to complete an activity and you give them 15, they will not take the time seriously next time.

5. Tell students up front why they are working in small groups. Tell them it is an important real-world skill and you want them to be highly successful in whatever they do. Tell them it is a privilege to get to work with other people instead of doing all the work alone. Tell them about synergy.

6. Sign up for instruction in cooperative learning techniques. You will learn a great deal about how to set up groups and how to manage them.

The third essential *communication is with parents.* Letters, notes, e-mail, phone calls, parent conferences, and group meetings are essential to maintaining a positive climate. In our restructured school we had a VIP (Very Important Parents) committee. This committee helped to create an open-door policy for parents and was the catalyst for setting up parent meetings—both individual and group. Parents were welcome and were encouraged to sit in classrooms at any time. Our only requirement was that the parents sign up in advance with our VIP chairman. This last requirement was for safety, so that we always knew who was in our building. An interesting thing happens when parents are in classrooms and hallways—discipline problems are diminished. An added benefit is that those parents become advocates in the community. We never held staff development sessions that parents were not invited to attend. I believe that is why we were able to make such radical changes in such a short amount of time. Anytime someone in the community said, "I don't know what they are doing at that school," there was someone who had been to the meetings, to the school, or in the training who could speak for us.

Fourth, *communication between the teacher and other staff members* is important to the overall climate of the building. Teachers need the opportunity to work with each other just as students do. It is difficult to set a classroom climate that is positive if the climate outside the classroom is negative. Unless administration is supportive, teachers will have a difficult time creating a collaborative environment. I have known situations where this was done, but the individual teachers spent many exhausting and frustrating days and nights to make it happen.

In our restructured school, teachers met daily in small teams to discuss a variety of topics. This time was built into the school day. Each team of teachers was responsible for 100 students. They were responsible for seeing whether any of them were absent too often, having discipline problems, or in danger of failure. Students with problems were called in to meet with the whole team. Teachers also discussed assignments for the week.

It is difficult to understand why some nights kids have no homework and other nights they are stressed over an unrealistic amount of work. Communication can help solve that problem. Teachers who meet daily can discuss upcoming assignments and work together on making them more evenly spaced. This is also the way to integrate learning. There are so many natural ways to connect one subject to another, *natural* meaning that the connection is already there—it does not have to be forced. In our restructured school, the more integrations we made, the more we found. As a result, math, science, English, and social studies became naturally aligned.

**In conclusion:** Where multiple communication is present in the classroom, interaction will be evident. Students will be actively discussing with the teacher and with each other. Newmann and Wehlage (1993) say that this interaction should include "indicators of higher order thinking such as making distinctions, applying ideas, forming generalizations, raising questions, and not just reporting experiences, facts, definitions or procedures."

In addition, in a multiple communication classroom, the teacher will act as a catalyst to the learning, not as the living textbook. Newmann and Wehlage (1993) add, "Sharing of ideas is evident in exchanges that are not completely scripted or controlled (as in a teacher-led recitation). Sharing is best illustrated when participants explain themselves or ask questions in complete sentences and when they respond directly to comments of previous speakers." Students will be provided numerous opportunities to work together to practice the learning, to develop concepts, to discuss ideas, and to produce quality products. Mutual respect will be evident in the verbal and non-verbal communication of the teacher and the students. Students will be actively engaged, not passive receivers of the information. Moreover, risk taking will be encouraged and supported. The teacher as well as the students will be risk takers with the learning. Social skills will be a part of the learning and assessment process. SCANS (U.S. Department of Labor, 1991) puts collaborative skills right up there with math and reading, so they should be given importance in the classroom not just because they are a skill for the marketplace but because they are a skill for life. Projects and assignments should clearly indicate that effective collaboration has taken place.

Teachers and administration should have active, ongoing communication with parents—an integral part of the process. In this multiply communicative school, every day is open house, for an open-door policy will exist that allows parents to visit the classroom and to communicate with teachers and staff whenever needed.

**FIGURE 6.2.** Indicators of a Classroom in Which Collaboration Is an Integral Part of the Learning

| Assessment Tools | Indicators of Success |
| --- | --- |
| Observations | Indicate interaction is a part of the classroom and that the interaction follows the precepts of Newmann and Wehlage (1993), who say that interaction should include higher-order thinking skills such as making distinctions, applying ideas, forming generalizations, raising questions, and not just reporting experiences, facts, definitions, or procedures |
| Observations | Indicate that the teacher acts as a catalyst to the learning, not as a living textbook |
| Lesson plans and observations | Indicate that students are provided numerous opportunities to work together to practice the learning, to develop concepts, to discuss ideas, and to produce quality products |
| Observations | Mutual respect will be evident in the verbal and nonverbal communication between the teacher and the students |
| Observations, student products | Students will be actively engaged, not passive receivers of the information |
| Observations, student assessment | There is an expectation that students will master social skills |
| Projects and assignments | Clearly indicate that effective collaboration has taken place |
| Climate surveys | Indicate that teachers and administration have active on-going communication |
| Parent surveys | Indicate that parents feel that they are a part of the process. An open-door policy exists to allow parents to visit the classroom and to communicate with teachers and staff. |

Figure 6.2 shows the indicators that will be present when multiple communication is present in the classroom.

# *Bridging the Gap Between All Learners, Regardless of Race, Socioeconomic Status, Sex, or Creed*

*We understand that every student cannot be brilliant. Each student, however, can enjoy a measure of success on his or her own terms that represents solid achievement and genuine accomplishment in completing substantial and meaningful academic work.*

—National Association of Secondary School
Principals (1996), *Breaking Ranks*

*Effective teachers say and do things which sincerely lead students to believe that it is their classroom, their learning, their activities that matter and that define success.*

—Haberman (1996),
"Characteristics of Star Teachers"

The time has come to quit assuming that all students come to us with the background to be successful in school. They do not. Ruby Payne (1996) wrote a stirring article for *The Instructional Leader* in which she discussed the hidden rules of cultures. The hidden rules "are the unspoken clueing systems that individuals use to indicate membership in a group." If we are ever to reach every student, if we are ever to have a 100% success rate, we must heighten our awareness of the cultural differences in the classroom and how they affect learning and behavior. Payne (1996) says,

One of the most important patterns is the following: In middle class, work and achievement tend to be the driving forces in decision making. In wealthy, the driving forces are the political, social, and financial connections. In generational poverty, the driving forces are survival, entertainment, and relationships.

She uses the example of a student whose Halloween costume costs $30 but whose book bill is not paid. She says, "Relationships and entertainment are more important than achievement" (Payne, 1996). We cannot bridge the gap between students until we understand what made the gap.

In order to provide a bridge for students, there are some factors that must be present; we must get away from isolation practices. I have been in more than a few classrooms where minority students or students whose primary language is different are seated at the back of the room or in isolation from the rest of the classroom. Move their desks to the front of the room and in proximity to the other students. They need the interaction and the attention.

Second, we must build relationships. Payne (1996) says,

For students from generational poverty to learn, a significant relationship must be present. When individuals who made it out of poverty were interviewed, virtually all cite an individual who made a significant difference for them. Not only must the relationship be present, but the academic tasks need to be referenced in terms of relationships.

As I stated in Chapter 1, we can raise the IQ level of students by as much as 20 points just by the climate we create.

Third, we must teach students the social skills they will need to be successful in the world they will enter. Part of the hidden rules is that different cultures are taught to react differently in stress situations. Children from generational poverty are taught to laugh in the face of adversity so that they do not show fear. Payne (1996) explains that a student who laughs when disciplined, however, will face further discipline. Schools tend to be built around middle-class standards that require a change in behavior and contriteness after discipline. I do not advocate that we accept laughter after discipline as OK, but I do believe that we need to educate students about what is the expected behavior. This is an important lesson if these students are to be successful in a world that is built around middle-class rules. As Payne (1996) says, "The recommended approach is simply to teach the student that he needs a set of rules that bring success in school and work and a set that brings success outside of school."

Fourth, we must desegregate state and national norm tests to be sure that no individual group is being overlooked academically. Often when scores are high for a group, the low scores of a single small group can be masked. We must not be content with scores until all groups are successful.

Fifth, where the cognitive structures are not in place, we must take the time to provide them. I have already discussed the importance of building

**FIGURE 7.1.** The J Curve

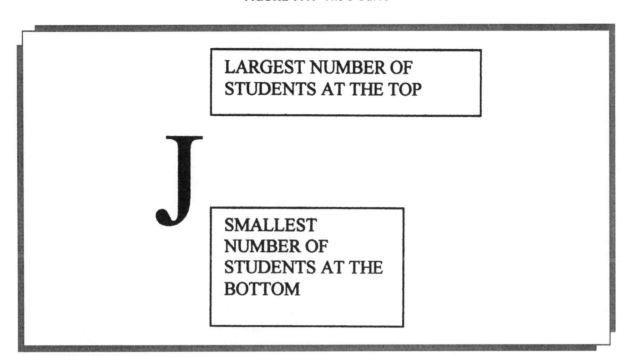

brain connections (see Chapter 3). We cannot assume that any student already has the cognitive structure in place to connect the new learning. We must find out if the structure is there and, if not, we must provide it.

No longer can we be resigned to saying that some students just won't be successful. Whose child are we willing to sacrifice? Mine? Yours? *Breaking Ranks* (NASSP, 1996) says,

> Teachers must prepare themselves to take on the challenge of lifting the learning levels of students whose failures have been lamented but accepted. Right now, it is a given that some students will learn and some will not. High schools tend to let everyone squeeze by— even most of those who are actually learning very little of an academic nature—as if moving on a conveyor belt. But the reality of American education is that some students are embarked upon a trip to nowhere.

The bell curve assumes that a few students will be highly successful, a few will fail, and the majority will fall somewhere in between. That has never made sense to me. If we are pouring money and effort into the low end, and for that matter, the high end, why do we still have a bell curve? Shouldn't the bell curve be an indication of what to expect before intervention? We should, instead, be getting something that looks more like a J-curve, with the vast majority at the high end.

**FIGURE 7.2.** Indicators That the Gap Between All Learners Has Been Bridged

| Assessment Tools | Indicators of Success |
|---|---|
| Test data | Will be analyzed for trends, highs, lows, and for each represented group |
| Observations | Relationships will be a priority in the classroom |
| Student products | Indicate that instruction has been designed to solicit, incorporate, and build upon the knowledge, experiences, and perspectives of all students |
| Staff training | Indicates that teachers stay abreast of latest trends and methodologies for all student groups |

**In conclusion:** When efforts are consciously made to bridge the gap between all learners, test data on students will be analyzed from a variety of perspectives. The data will be massaged for trends, highs, lows, and for each represented group. Teachers and staff will stay abreast of the latest research on how students learn through staff development and education literature. In addition, the teacher will use direct teaching techniques to help provide cognitive structures where none exist. Perhaps most important, the climate in the classroom will be, at all times, a supportive and nurturing one where building relationships is a priority and where there will be no hidden agendas.

Figure 7.2 shows the indicators that will be present when all students are successful.

# Evaluating Learning Through a Variety of Authentic Assessments

*Retrieved memories are the only evidence we have of learning.*
—Marilee Springer (1999), *Learning and Memory*

In Chapter 4, I discussed the five memory compartments of the brain. They are semantic, which holds memory learned from words; episodic, which deals with locations of the learning; procedural, which remembers processes that the body performs; automatic, which deals with learning that is a conditioned response; and emotional, which is given priority in the brain. Assessment should be a procedure to retrieve information from students' long-term memory using the various retrieval compartments of the brain. By doing this, teachers will have a more accurate measure of what students have placed in long-term memory.

Assessment should also truly reflect what students need to be able to do with the learning. To do all this, schools must ask some hard questions about the assessment. Does the assessment provide adequate information about the degree of learning? What is the appropriate vehicle for the assessment? Has adequate time been allowed to ensure that assessment of long-term memory is taking place, not just memorization for the short term? What is important to measure? Do we need to measure the process, the product, or both? More important, does the assessment truly reflect the learning? Is it more important that students are able to name the date of the Yalta Agreement or that they know the process to find that date should they need it?

Assessment should be an active demonstration of student understanding and their ability to apply this understanding. Marlowe and Page (1998) tell us,

> To create assessment instruments that do more than merely tap a student's recall or recognition skills, we must reframe assessment so that

- It is, as much as possible, a continuous process that is part of instruction and not separate from it

- It connects directly to learning and is introduced before or simultaneously with material

- It requires students to do more than simply remember (e.g., requires students to develop mathematical formulas, produce exhibitions, write essays, create a sculpture, write poetry, create a musical score, develop and participate in debates, or create and conduct experiments)

- Student questions, at least in part, drive the process

When we have authentic teaching, we have teaching that mirrors the concepts, generalizations, facts, and processes that students need to know and be able to do in the real world, then it follows that the assessment should be authentic. By authentic, I mean that the assessment truly measures the students' understanding and ability to use the learning and that the learning is in long-term memory.

Newmann and Wehlage (1993) identify authentic achievement as "achievement that is significant and meaningful" as compared to that which is "trivial and useless." They use three criteria to define authentic achievement:

1. Students construct meaning and produce knowledge

2. Students use disciplined inquiry to construct meaning

3. Students aim their work toward production of discourse, products, or performances that have value or meaning beyond success in school

Using the criteria provided by Newmann and Wehlage (1993), let's examine authentic assessment. First, schools should assess a student's ability to construct meaning and produce knowledge. In a constructivist classroom, students are given opportunities to construct meaning based on the connections already present in their brains. A student who truly understands the learning can use the learning in new situations, problems, or structures other than those in which the information was produced. It is one thing to learn a mathematical operation one week and be able to use it in the problems assigned, and another to gain the ability to determine which operation to use at a later date when a set of problems is given. If the pattern or connection is in long-term memory, the student should be able to pull from it a week or month later. Jenson (1998) says that we cannot truly assess knowledge until at least 24 hours after the instruction. Anything assessed sooner may be in a short-term situation. He uses the example of going to a phone booth and looking up a phone number. We remember it just long enough to use the number. If we need the same number again the next day, the chances are that we will have to look it up again.

Second, how do we know that students can use disciplined inquiry to construct meaning? Ron Brandt (1993), in an interview with Howard Gardner, offered the following:

> As long as you are determined to cover everything, you actually insure that most kids are not going to understand. You've got to take enough time to get kids deeply involved in something so they can think about it in lots of different ways and apply it—not just at school but at home and on the street and so on.

There is no way that we can teach students everything they need to know in order to be successful. First of all, we don't know what will be necessary for them to know in their lifetimes to be successful. We must give them tools to formulate understanding, structures for problem solving, and research retrieval skills and then we must assess to see if they can use these tools. We do that by giving them assessment exercises that employ these processes. Independent projects, experiments, and complex problem solving are some of the ways this can be accomplished.

Third, products and performances are at a quality level and have meaning. We discussed in Chapter 5 the importance of setting high expectations for student products. The teacher needs to set the standard high and give specific parameters for the expected project. While it is important to give students choices, it is equally important to set parameters to ensure that the final product reflects quality. Instead of saying to students that we want a research project on the brain and learning, we might say instead that we want a research project on the brain and learning that includes at a minimum the work of Jenson, Sousa, and Sylwester. We might also let them choose the format of the finished product. For example, the finished product might be written as a monograph on the need for changes in education, presented in a multimedia format using PowerPoint,® or dramatized as a student forum. Students have choices, but the teacher sets the parameters for the level of quality. The highest level a product can attain is that of providing usefulness beyond the person who created it.

Whenever I think about quality products, I am reminded of an experience that I had with my own son. In the school that we restructured, we decided as a faculty that we would accept only quality work. We took to heart Deming's words, "Do it right the first time and every time," and we made believers of our students. In the past, our gifted students had not been truly challenged. They could usually slop something together and turn it in for an "A" because it was still better than what the other students were turning in. But this was a new year and our expectations were higher for those "other kids." Our students who had traditionally not done well in school were suddenly turning in quality work, and whenever you raise the floor, you have to raise the ceiling. So for the first time, gifted students were truly being challenged to do work at a higher level. One afternoon I came home from work to find my own son, who was in the gifted program, working diligently on a project for English class. He was studying British literature and he was creating a shield fashioned after the shields used in England that depicted information about the family that bore them. Each section of the shield was to depict different characteristics of his beliefs and heritage. I had a parent meeting to go to so I left him working in the living room. I wasn't much concerned about the state of the living room with his materials strewed everywhere because I knew he would be finished by the time I returned. His group of friends adhered to the 15-minute rule on homework. If it was going to take more than 15 minutes, they would get on the phone and divide up the work. They were into cooperative learning long before we added it to the curriculum. Imagine my surprise when I returned about 9:30 to find that he was still busy at the project. I took one look at the living room and said, "Kevin, just push all this stuff to the side, we'll clean it up tomorrow. I want to go to bed." He frowned. "I can't, I'm not finished with my shield. There is one part that I can't do. I know what I want to say but I can't draw it. It's the part about my political view and if I tell you what I want to say will you draw it for me?" Now I have a limited amount of artistic ability—I mainly draw only for family and friends—so on most nights I would not have minded the task. However, I had been up since 6 that morning, I had worked all day, and I had met with parents that night. So I said, "Just cut something out of a magazine and paste it on, I want to go to bed." He replied, "You don't understand, it's a matter of quality!" We had saved one gifted child.

Lessons should begin with the end in mind. What is important for students to know and understand? Grant Wiggins and Jay McTighe (1998) describe a lesson design that looks at performance first. Before teachers build the lesson, they ask these critical questions:

- What enabling knowledge (facts, concepts, and principles) and skills (procedures) will students need to perform effectively to achieve desired results?

- What activities will equip students with the needed knowledge and skills?

- What will need to be taught and coached, and how should it best be taught, in light of performance goals?

- What materials and resources are best suited to accomplish these goals?

- Is the overall design coherent and effective?

Evaluation should be both formative and summative. Formative evaluations should be ongoing and frequent. Jenson (1995) says that students who lack sufficient feedback (at least once every 30 minutes) will either go out of their way to get attention (pester the teacher or be a discipline problem) or will simply lose interest in the class and check out. Formative evaluations are benchmarks by which the teacher and student check to see that the student understands and is working at a pace and level that will ensure success. Formative evaluations should be carried out by both the teacher and the student. Jenson (1995) says, "We all may be accidentally retarding thinking, intelligence and brain growth, and ultimately creating slow learners by the lack of feedback and the large lag time we have built into the typical learning environment." He also advocates that students need to evaluate their own learning. He continues, "Most great thinkers of history like Leonardo da Vinci have kept elaborate journals of their work. That was their self feedback."

Summative evaluations should evaluate the students' understanding of material presented and their ability to use it not only in the context in which it was taught, but in other contexts as well. Summative evaluations should be closely woven into the learning process. Ellis and Fouts (1997) say, "In a more perfect educational world, it would be impossible to separate assessment procedures from curriculum content." If assessment is authentic, it should be closely aligned to the day-to-day experiences of the curriculum.

**In conclusion:** In a classroom where authentic assessment is practiced, students will demonstrate understanding by being able to use the learning in different contexts. They will produce meaningful products that move beyond personal success, and the assessments will follow a wide range of choices. Students will be able to use a variety of inquiry skills to solve problems, create products, and access information. Assessments will reflect the learning, be tied to the rubric or guidelines for success, and will not be a surprise to the learners. Assessments will demonstrate learning beyond state and national standards and will incorporate high-level, complex knowledge.

Figure 8.1 shows indicators that will be present when authentic assessment is practiced.

**FIGURE 8.1.** Indicators That a Variety of Assessments
That Authentically Evaluate the Learner Are Used

| Assessment Tools | Indicators of Success |
|---|---|
| Student products | Demonstrate understanding by being able to use the learning in different contexts |
| Student products | Indicate student use of a variety of inquiry skills to solve problems, create products, and access information |
| Student assessments | Indicate a wide range, reflect the learning, and follow the rubric |
| Student assessments | Indicate learning beyond state and national standards |

# Promoting Real-World Application of the Learning

*Our curriculum is worthless if we cannot convince students that they are learning useful life skills.*

—W. Glasser, 1994: "Teach Students
What They Will Need in Life"

Sousa (1995) says that there seem to be two main questions asked in working memory to determine whether information should move to long-term memory or be tossed out. The first question that he addresses has to do with whether the information makes sense; that is, whether there is enough prior information or experience to which to attach the new information so that the learner can understand it. It is the second question that he says is the most important to long-term memory. That is the question of whether the new learning is relevant. He says that traditional schools spend a great deal of time on making sense of the learning but very little on making the learning relevant. Thus, students can often perform tasks in class one day but cannot recall them the next.

Most students can be taught anything as long as it is relevant to their world. Glasser (cited in Gough, 1993) says that is why young children learn one of the most difficult things to learn, they learn a language, and no one stands in front of them with flash cards. One of my favorite math teachers has a sign in her room that should be in every classroom in America. It says, "I promise I will never teach you anything in this classroom unless I can tell you how you are going to use it in the real world." And she is true to her word. When her students studied slope, she talked about how slope is important to the specifications of handicap ramps. Then, she and her students went into the community to measure handicap ramps to see if they met the criteria. When they studied angles, she had a member of the Texas Highway Commission talk to her class about angled parking. Her class measured and set the specifications for some of the angled parking in her town.

John Bruer (1993) says, "Students need to play with the new information they have acquired and manipulated in authentic situations to develop genuine understanding. Until they are given chances to construct and make the information meaningful in their own lives, the learning remains superficial and ephemeral."

How, then, do we ensure that real-world application is a part of the learning? First, we tie the learning to something the student already knows about. In the examples above, the teacher took some pretty abstract concepts, such as slope and angles, and gave them concrete connections. Another important connector for memory is patterns. We know that if we can create a connection to a pattern already present in the brain, it is more likely that students will remember. The teacher took concepts with which the students were already somewhat familiar—ramps and parking—and connected the concepts of slope and angles.

When English students were studying Beowulf, they talked about the monsters that people believed in at that time. The teacher asked, "Are there modern-day monsters?" She assigned the students a project. They were to bring to class a representation of a modern-day monster. The representations had to be visual with a written narrative. The depth of the student products was remarkable. One student brought his monster to class, and he read,

> In the book of Acts, we are told that the Apostle Paul had a "thorn in the flesh." We are never told exactly what it was. Theologians and historians have theorized that it was a pain or incurable disease that would not go away. But, I disagree. I think, instead, that it was the monster of memory. Perhaps it was the memory of the faces of the Christians that he killed before his conversion. I have recently met a man who was decorated for bravery in the Vietnam War, but he sleeps only four hours each night because he is haunted by the memory of the faces of the people he had to kill. My grandfather went to high school with one of the men who dropped the bomb on Hiroshima. He lives today in a mental institution, forever frozen in time. When my grandfather goes to visit him, he thinks they are still in high school and wants to know what they are going to do on Saturday night for fun.

I believe this student knows far more about the monsters that each generation has had to face than he would had we had him memorize places, characters, and passages, yet never talked about the real-world application. Real-world application reaches into the depth of understanding; it is far more than just covering the material. We hope that students will become more productive and reflective as a result.

The other dimension of real-world application is reflection. We need to provide opportunities for students to reflect on the learning. Opportunities are given for students to think about what they have learned, its significance,

**FIGURE 9.1.** Indicators That Instruction Promotes
Real-World Application of the Learning

| Assessment Tools | Indicators of Success |
| --- | --- |
| Lesson plans | Indicate that the knowledge has been applied to authentic situations that occur outside the classroom as well as within |
| Journals and student products | Indicate depth of understanding and opportunities for reflection |
| Assessments | Indicate students' understanding of real-world application |

and what that has to do with their world. By doing that, we give the learning relevance and an emotional attachment. Both of those phenomena help ensure long-term memory. In my book (Walker, 1998) I talk about a technique that I use in the classroom to facilitate reflection. It is called What, So What, and Now What. Students fill out the What (have you learned) section first. I give ample time for true reflection and I don't accept shallow answers. Next, students fill out the section titled, So What (difference does it make). In this section, students tell why the leaning was important. Last, students fill out the Now What (can I do with it) section by giving examples of how it can be used in their world.

Caine and Caine (1991) said,

> Much of the effort put into teaching and studying is wasted because students do not adequately process their experiences. What we call active processing allows students to review how and what they learned so that they begin to take charge of learning and the development of personal meanings. In part, active processing refers to reflection in metacognitive activities.

**In conclusion:** In a classroom where real-world application to the learning is actually applied, there will be evidence in the lesson that the knowledge has been connected to authentic situations that occur outside the classroom as well as within. Moreover, students will be given opportunities to reflect on the learning as evidenced by journals and written guided reflections. Depth of understanding will be evident through journals, products, and written materials, and part of assessment will be the student's ability to tie the learning to real-world situations.

Figure 9.1 shows the indicators that will be present when real-world application is applied to the learning.

# Seamless Integration of Technology for High-Quality Instruction

*There are thousands of buildings in this country, with millions of people in them who have no telephones, no cable television, and no reasonable prospect of broadband services—they're called schools.*

—Reed Hundt, Chairman,
Federal Communications Commission

Students enter our school hallways each day fresh from a digital world that not only allows them to communicate throughout the world but gives them the ability to problem solve, do research, and perform at levels never before available in the history of man. Those same students often go to classrooms where the primary learning tools are lecture, note taking, and rote learning. No wonder they drop out mentally.

Schools cannot be held totally to blame for the slow move to high-end technology. State and local governments that hold the purse strings for school finance have been reluctant to fund the hardware and software costs involved in bringing schools into this century. Many schools lack adequate wiring to support technology, and massive building expenses mean higher taxes. Unfortunately, many of the technology decisions of the past were based on limited knowledge and relied far too heavily on drill and practice software rather than the productivity tools that mirror the real world.

Dr. William Banach (1998), in his annual list of "What's Hot and What's Not," talks about the fact that technology has given students a whole new range of choices. He says, "Forward thinkers are imagining what learning will look like when education comes through air, so that anyone can learn anything, anywhere, any time." He goes on to say that students will be able to "choose to take biology on the Internet, math from a virtual university, business communication from a corporate college, and current events" all from home.

Allen Schmieder, in an interview with Jean Shields (1999) for *Curriculum Administrator*, says,

> Schools are three knowledge generations behind reality. There is no content out there or a system in place to connect schools to cutting edge research. Schools need to reflect society. Imagine jobs in math and science without technology. The chance we have in technology is to analyze problems differently, to create new ways of knowing.

The International Technology Education Association's (ITEA) Technology for All Americans Project (TfAAP) is developing a set of content standards for technology education set to be released in 2000. The project is funded by the National Science Foundation and the National Aeronautics and Space Administration. Its goal, according to William Dugger (1999), Director of the International Technology Education Association's Technology for All Americans Project, is to "promote excellence in technology education by defining the domain of technology, promoting the study of technology, and creating standards." He defines technology education as "a tool to enhance the process of teaching and learning." He warns that technology education is very different from educational technology, which deals primarily with the delivery of instruction using technology in the classroom. While this chapter will deal with both technology education and educational technology, a more in-depth understanding of what is meant by technology education is needed here. Educational technology involves three organizers: processes, knowledge, and contexts. Processes include any human activities that "create, invent, design, transform, produce, control, maintain, or use products and systems." Knowledge encompasses those things that deal with "how technological content is developed and applied." Contexts include those larger areas where technology is "developed, applied, and studied." All three components are mutually dependent. "With technological knowledge, people engage in the processes; it is through the processes that humans solve problems and extend their capabilities. Contexts are larger macrosystems where technology is organized" (Dugger, 1999).

In the preceding chapters, nine best practices were discussed. All of these practices can be greatly enhanced by the use of good technology. As a matter of fact, technology is the vehicle that can help shift classrooms to best practices.

In Chapter 1, climate and its powerful effect on student learning were discussed. Through the use of technology, teachers will be more effectively able to monitor and provide anytime, anywhere assistance to students. Through Internet and Intranet resources, students will be able to get assignments, additional help, and clarifications on-line. Students who are absent or unable to attend classes can learn on-line. Students will have more choices as a whole world of learning opportunities becomes available. Telementoring will be the wave of the future as students are linked to adults with like interests and abilities through e-mail. Ann Foster (1999) quotes a 1995 Impact Study of Big Brothers/Big Sisters of America that shows that, "Young people with mentors are 46 percent less likely to begin using illegal drugs, 27 percent less likely to begin using alcohol, 53 percent less likely to skip school, 37 percent less likely to skip a class, and 33 percent less likely to hit someone." A mentor who can be accessed anytime, anywhere is a step forward from the mentoring programs of the past that took place only on certain days of the week and at specified times.

In Chapter 2, the need to address the various learning styles of students was outlined. Much software is available to the classroom today that incorporates visual, verbal, and kinesthetic learning. Software tools allow the teacher who is unfamiliar with visual models to create them easily and effortlessly just by plugging in his or her teaching outline. Students who need visuals to learn, students who are dyslexic and need graphic representations, will be able to view the learning in a format that is comfortable and meaningful to them. Lessons can be more interesting with the addition of multimedia formats that more closely mirror the world from which our students come. Just adding PowerPoint® presentations to low technology tools such as chalkboard and overheads would add a new dimension to teaching and learning.

In Chapter 3, I discussed the need to help students make connections from prior learning to the new learning. Through technology, students will be able to view the learning as well as hear it. They will also have the opportunity individually to review past information. Through the use of animation and visuals, teachers will be able to give the learning relevance to a degree not possible in the past. Talking about polar bears to children who live in southern regions has much less relevance than taking them through virtual classrooms to a zoo or region where they can see real polar bears. Technology opens up a whole new world of learning to those students who need visual representations. I recently volunteered to read to a group of first graders in a school near me. When the teacher brought the children to the library for the lesson, she sat one child off to the side by himself. She whispered to me that he would probably not sit quietly for the lesson and that she was placing him so that she could easily remove him from the room if necessary. Instead of just reading the book to the children, as we so often do, I read the book as I showed selected pictures from the story using PowerPoint® software and an LCD projection device that showed the pictures on my computer on a television monitor. Not only did the young man in question sit quietly for the story, but when I had finished, he yelled, "Do it again!" This was a visual child in an auditory world and he had already become a discipline problem in first grade because he was being forced to learn in a modality not comfortable for him.

At a Ranger baseball game, I was amazed at the powerful teaching tools that were used on the huge multimedia screen in the park. Points came across easily and in short periods of time with the video clips, animated words, and pictures that flashed often across the screen. A long ball to right field might bring an animated "Wow" on the screen. The productivity tools are available now to make dynamic, exciting presentations in the classroom. An emotional "Wow" every once in a while would be good for us all.

In Chapter 4, the need to help students put the information into long-term memory rather than just memorizing for a test was addressed. The sensory devices that are a part of technology will allow teachers to enrich their lessons for the classroom. Research projects have greater relevance when students encounter information and concepts through virtual classrooms, distance learning, the Internet, and worldwide e-mail. Student projects take on a new dimension with technology as their guide. Semantic memory will be enhanced by technology because relevance or meaning will be more evident as students are able to apply information to authentic situations and problems. Student projects can be created virtually so that immediate relevance is seen rather than having to wait until a time in the future when students have jobs that deal with real problems.

Teachers can enhance episodic memory by using technology to create props or tools that trigger recall. A prop as simple as a red tennis shoe created by technology to prompt students to remember the rules for using verbs is a simple example of how episodic memory can be enhanced through technology.

In Chapter 5, the importance of teaching to higher-level thinking in the classroom was addressed. Technology assists with this by providing a rich environment for research. The possibilities are limitless. By using good productivity tools, the quality of products that students can produce is enhanced. Written reports take on a new dimension when the student is able to add animation and other visuals in a PowerPoint® or similar presentation. An added bonus is that with technology, students can work on their project anytime, anywhere rather than having to rely on the office hours of libraries or museums. A group of high school students used technology to study the force of motion on roller coasters to set up their rides and then measure the g-forces. This type of experiment would not be possible without technology, since human subjects could experience whiplash or worse while the project was in its experimental stages.

In Chapter 6, the need for collaboration was emphasized. Technology opens all the windows and doors to make this possible. Parents may not be able to come to the school, but the school can come to them through e-mail, the Internet, distance learning, and virtual classes. Schools can communicate better with all of the stakeholders through virtual opportunities. Student projects and studies will not be limited to the students in the classroom. Students can work with other students in the building and in other schools as well. Teachers can communicate with each other literally anytime, anywhere. Collaboration takes on a whole new meaning with technology.

The need to reach 100% of the students was revealed in Chapter 7. Technology is the tool that will lead the way to making education equitable for all students, regardless of their background. The computer does not see race, wealth, gender, or beliefs. It is a great equalizer. The hidden agendas of society are not a factor there. Schools that need and want to bridge the gap should be actively pursuing the resources to make high-level technology possible. Governments that tout high standards must come to realize that high standards require high-level tools. The future of education rests on two things. First, quality teachers who can not only teach in the traditional classroom but in a non-traditional setting as well, and who can inspire. Second, technology that is of a high level and that mirrors the real world. These are the gateways to produce a quality product.

The authentic assessments in Chapter 8 take on a higher level of quality when we add productivity tools. Students will also be able to create electronic portfolios and logs that help track and showcase growth. An electronic portfolio is probably a better tool for university and job applications than the traditional test scores and grades. If completed properly, the portfolios show the multitalents of the individual rather than the single ability to take tests.

Nothing is more real world than the experience of being in the place discussed, conversing with the people being studied, or watching practitioners use the skills being learned. Through video conferencing, virtual classrooms, distance learning, and the Internet, all of these things are possible today.

These are not ideas for the future—I do not consider myself to be a futurist. These are the possibilities of now. Education should be so exciting, so exacting, that students would literally run to get to it. Technology will help make this a reality.

**In conclusion:** Schools that place a priority on technology provide technology that is accessible to everyone, all day, not just in laboratory situations. Both instructional technology, which deals with creating an optimum teaching and learning environment, and educational technology, which deals with technology literacy, are a vital part of the curriculum. The emphasis is on using productivity tools, not expensive drill and practice software, and student products reflect the use of these tools.

At a minimum, these schools provide access to the Internet, Intranet, and e-mail for teachers and students. Students learn processes that reflect technology use at a high level. Some examples are PowerPoint presentations beginning in elementary school, e-mail for student collaboration at all levels, and Web authoring by the secondary level. School Internet resources allow parents to retrieve information about student assignments, progress, and curriculum anytime.

Classes will not be limited to a single space or to a single building, but will be opened up to the possibilities of distance learning. Through technol-

**FIGURE 10.1.** Indicators That Technology Is Used at a Quality Level

| Assessment Tools | Indicators of Success |
| --- | --- |
| Observation | Technology tools will be accessible to everyone |
| Observation | Technology will be integrated into the classroom, not relegated to an isolated lab setting |
| Student products | Indicate an emphasis on productivity tools, not expensive drill and practice software |
| Technology tools | Indicate that students and teachers have access to the Internet, Intranet, and e-mail |
| Student products | Indicate learning processes that reflect technology use at a high level |
| Parent surveys | Indicate access to school Internet and Intranet services to retrieve information from student assignments, progress, and curriculum anytime |
| Field trips | Reflect virtual trips to places heretofore not accessible to the school |
| Class offerings | Indicate that they are not limited by a single space or a single building but offer possibilities through the Internet, distance learning, and video conferencing |
| Student products | Will indicate that students have been taught the elements of information retrieval, including the ability to discern between primary and secondary resources, the difference between fact and opinion, and the ethics of using technology responsibly |
| Lessons | Indicate the use of technology to make them more dynamic, emotional, and relevant |

ogy, students will be able to take classes never before possible. The lines between school and college will be blurred as students take college and career courses along with their basic skills classes for high school graduation.

Through technology, the classroom takes on another dimension as the world—rather than the bricks-and-mortar building—becomes the classroom. Resources never before possible, relevance and depth of study at a level never before achieved in a classroom, and the exchange of ideas with unlimited possibilities boggle the mind. Technology is not an end in itself, but it can lead us toward the type of classroom we have all dreamed about.

Figure 10.1 shows the indicators that will be present when technology is utilized at a quality level.

# Putting It All Together 11

"All men dream": but not equally. Those who dream by night in
the dusty recesses of their mind wake in the day to find that it was
vanity: but the dreamers of the day are dangerous men, for they
may act their dream with open eyes, to make it possible.

—E. E. Lawrence, *Seven Pillars of Wisdom*

These 10 teaching strategies provide a framework for a change in the way
we view teaching and learning. We cannot dismiss the knowledge of
how the brain works nor the information on learning styles. To do so would
be folly and a disaster to education. We cannot close our ears to the cry for
standards; they are a part of the accountability world in which we live. We
cannot go on believing that we don't need to change, that it is the children
who need to change. As the world has changed, so have our students. Now it
is our turn; education must move into the new millennium

The past millennium was about standards; this one should be about
putting quality practices into place. *A Nation at Risk*, the report of the National
Commission on Excellence in Education (1983), chaired by then Secretary of
Education, Terrell Bell, boldly said that schools were held directly responsible
for the downward spiral of the United States as an industrial leader and that
the erosion of educational standards "threatens our very future as a people."
That report became a pivot point in American education as it turned state,
local, and national government on its heels to race for more guidelines, more
testing, and more standards. The Association for Supervision and Curriculum Development (1999b), in its electronic newsletter, quoted convention
speaker Richard Strong, who said that we now have more than 4,000 standards nationally yet students can learn only 1,500 of them during their K-12
education.

All too often standards have limited, rather than enhanced, the progress of students. Teachers, fearful of low test scores on state and national tests, spend far too much time on drill and practice routines to get students ready for "the test." I do not mean to imply that I don't believe we need standards, quite the opposite. Shouldn't standards, however, be similar to setting parameters for student work? Standards should set the parameters for what students should know and be able to do. They should set the height from the floor (minimum expectations) to the possibilities for the ceiling (maximum expectations), for when we raise the floor, we need to raise the ceiling. Some standards already do that, but the vast majority are too specific and too limiting. How to teach has often focused on procedure or technical aspects rather than on standards of quality. While procedure is important, procedure without quality and authenticity does not lead to meaningful learning. Without quality processes, how can we expect quality products?

When we wanted to restructure our school, we called in the leaders of business and industry in our community and asked, "If we could give you a better product, would you pay for it?" The answer was a resounding "Yes." One company owner stood up and said not only would he be willing to pay for a quality product, but he would also pledge to release workers to sit on committees and task forces to help us make the dream possible.

He kept his word and we kept ours—we produced a quality product.

How, then, do we produce quality? The 10 teaching practices offered in this book are only a beginning, but an important beginning. The first time our students in the restructured school took our state test we were filled with anxiety. We had relied on higher-level thinking skills to drive our curriculum rather than spending mindless hours on drill and practice for the test as many of our neighbors were doing. After all, in our state and most others, test scores for each school are front-page news each spring. When the results came back, our students had done very well. Some of the students made a comment that I think of each time I hear the controversy about standards. They said, "We don't know why you were so uptight about our taking the test. The work we do every day is so much more difficult than anything on that test. Taking the test was easy in comparison." Maybe when we teach the complex skills needed by our students for the new millennium, the tests will take care of themselves. Neighboring schools had told us we were crazy to try to do so much so fast, but like the dreamers of the day, we listened to our own instincts and the pedagogy of what works for kids . . . and we made the dream a reality.

The strategies suggested in this book require a change in the way we view teaching and learning. Far too many still believe that it is the children, not education, that must change. The paradox is that children will not change until we change the way we teach them, the way we assess them, and the climate in which they learn. I began this book with a quote about the need to make exceptional learning unexceptional. It is time to make exceptional learning the norm.

# References

Association for Supervision and Curriculum Development. (1999a). *ASCD yearbook.* Alexandria, VA: Author.

Association for Supervision and Curriculum Development. (1999b). *Electronic Newsletter.* Alexandria, VA: Author.

Banach, W. J. (1998, Winter). What's hot and what's not. *TEPSA Journal,* pp. 8-9.

Barker, J. (1992). *Future edge.* New York: William Morrow.

Bloom, B. S. (1976). *Human characteristics and school learning.* New York: McGraw-Hill.

Brandt, R. (1993). On teaching for understanding: A conversation with Howard Gardner. *Educational Leadership, 50*(7), 3-7.

Bruer, J. T. (1993). *Schools for learning.* Cambridge: MIT Press.

Caine, R., & Caine, G. (1991). *Making connections: Teaching and the human brain.* Alexandria, VA: Association for Supervision and Curriculum Development.

Covey, S. R. (1989). *Seven habits of highly effective people.* New York: Simon & Schuster.

Diamond, M. (1988). *Enriching heredity: The impact of the environment on the anatomy of the brain.* New York: Free Press.

Diamond, M., & Hopson, J. (1998). *Magic trees of the mind.* New York: E. P. Dutton.

Diamond, M., Scheibel, A., Murphy, G., & Harvey, T. (1985). On the brain of a scientist: Albert Einstein. *Experimental Neurology, 88,* 198-204.

Dugger, W. E. (1999). Putting technology education standards into practice. *NASSP Bulletin* (Reston, VA: National Association of Secondary School Principals), *83*(608), 57-63.

Ellis, A. K., & Fouts, J. T. (1997). *Research and educational innovations.* Larchmont, NY: Eye on Education.

Feuerstein, R., et al. (1980). *Instrumental enrichment: An intervention program for cognitive modifiability.* Glenview, IL: Scott, Foresman.

Fitzgerald, R. (1996). Brain compatible teaching in the block schedule. *The School Administrator, 8*(2), 20.

Foster, A. (1999). Telementoring: One way to reach America's students. *NASSP Bulletin* (Reston, VA: National Association of Secondary School Principals), *83*(608), 76-79.

Glasser, W. (1994, March-April). Teach students what they will need in life. *ATPE News,* pp. 20-21.

Gough, P. B. (1993). The key to improving schools—An interview with William Glasser. *Phi Delta Kappan, 78*(8), 599.

Greenbough, W. T., & Anderson, B. J. (1991). Cerebellar synaptic plasticity: Relation to learning versus neural activity. *Annals of the New York Academy of Science, 627,* 231-247.

Haberman, M. (1996). Characteristics of star teachers. *Instructional Leader, 9*(6), 1-3.

Hanson, J. M., & Childs, J. (1998). Creating a school where people like to be. *Educational Leadership, 50*(1), 14-16.

Henderson, N., & Milstein, M. (1996). *Resiliency in schools: Making it happen for students and educators.* Thousand Oaks, CA: Corwin.

Jacoby, P. (1991). *Region XIII Education Service Center.* Austin, Texas: Author.

Jenson, E. (1995). *The learning brain.* Del Mar, CA: Turning Point.

Jenson, E. (1998). *Introduction to brain compatible learning.* Del Mar, CA: Turning Point.

Keefe, J. M. (1997). *Instruction and the learning environment.* Larchmont, NY: Eye on Education.

Kotulak, R. (1996). *Inside the brain.* Kansas City, MO: Andrews McMeel.

Marlowe, B. A., & Page, M. L. (1998). *Creating and sustaining the constructivist classroom.* Thousand Oaks, CA: Corwin.

National Association of Secondary School Principals. (1996). *Breaking ranks: Changing an American institution.* Reston, VA: Author.

National Commission on Excellence in Education. (1983). *A nation at risk: Imperative for educational reform.* Washington, DC: Government Printing Office.

Newmann, F. W., & Wehlage, G. G. (1993). Five standards of authentic instruction. *Educational Leadership, 50*(7), 8-12.

O'Neil, J. (1995). On lasting school reform: A conversation with Ted Sizer. *Educational Leadership, 52*(5), 12.

O'Tuel, F. S., & Bullard, P. K. (1993). *Developing higher order thinking in the content areas K-12.* Pacific Grove, CA: Critical Thinking Press.

Payne, R. (1996). Understanding and working with students and adults from poverty. *The Instructional Leader, 9*(2), 3-5.

Perry, B. D. (1995). *Children, youth, and violence: Seaching for solutions.* New York: Guilford.

Pyle, G., & Andre, T. (1986*). Cognitive classroom learning–Understanding thinking and problem solving.* Orlando, FL: Academic Press.

Resnick, O. P., & Resnick, L. B. (1997). The nature of literacy: An historical exploration. *Harvard Educational Review, 47*(3).

Shields, J. (1999). New ways of knowing: An interview with Allen Schmieder. *Curriculum Administrator, 35*(4), 68-70.

Sousa, D. (1995). *How the brain learns.* Reston, VA: National Association of Secondary School Principals.

Sousa, D. (1997). *How the brain learns: New insights into the teaching/learning process* [Audiotape]. Reston, VA: National Association of Secondary School Principals.

Sousa, D. (1999). *How the brain learns.* Reston, VA: National Association of Secondary School Principals.

Springer, M. (1999). *Learning and memory: The brain in action.* Alexandria, VA: Association for Supervision and Curriculum Development.

Toliver, K. (1995). *Good morning Mrs. Toliver* [Videotape]. Los Angeles, CA: KCET.

Torrence, E. P. (1966). *Torrence test of creative thinking.* Princeton, NJ: Personnel Press.

U.S. Department of Labor. (1991). *Scans: Blueprint for action.* Washington, DC: Author.

Walker, D. (1998). *Strategies for teaching differently: On the block or not.* Thousand Oaks, CA: Corwin.

Wayman, P. (1998). *Super teaching strategies.* Windsor, CA: Center for New Discoveries in Learning.

Werner, E. E., & Smith, R. S. (1992). *Overcoming the odds: High risk children from birth to adulthood.* Ithaca, NY: Cornell University Press.

Whisler, N., & Williams, J. (1990). *Literature and cooperative learning: Pathway to literacy.* Sacramento, CA: Literature Co-op. (Available from Literature Co-op, 2020 7th Avenue, Sacramento, CA 95818)

Wiggins, G., & McTighe, J. (1998). *Understanding by design.* Alexandria, VA: National Association for Supervision and Curriculum Development.

# Index

CORWIN
PRESS

**The Corwin Press logo**—a raven striding across an open book—represents the happy union of courage and learning. We are a professional-level publisher of books and journals for K–12 educators, and we are committed to creating and providing resources that embody these qualities. Corwin's motto is "Success for All Learners."